# Measuring Up in Education

Cultures of measurement are often considered to dominate educational practices, to the degree that, as Biesta (2010) has identified in *Good Education in an Age of Measurement* we no longer measure what we value, but rather we have become conditioned to value what is measured. A clear example of this occurs when institutions and staff "teach to the test" by emphasising narrow conceptions of learning and of knowledge, simply because the consequences of high-stakes assessments have important implications regarding funding, resources, and even tenure.

This collection explores, via various philosophical means, how valuable educational practices can occur within and beyond cultures of measurement. What seems to be required is for practitioners in education to regain their relationship to the overall purposes of education, such as the furthering of justice and democracy for both individual students and societies as a whole. Such a reconnection has the potential to re-humanise curricular experiences for students, which may have become dehumanised through particular cultures of measurement. It is argued that certain legitimate measures can advance justice and democracy, and so careful attention must be assigned to their validity and value.

This book was originally published as a special issue of *Educational Philosophy and Theory*.

**Steven A. Stolz, PhD,** is a Senior Lecturer at La Trobe University, Australia. He has a diverse array of research interests, which ranges from: critical theory, epistemology, phenomenology, embodied cognition, narrative inquiry, and learning theories in psychology. At the moment, his primary area of scholarship is concerned with the relationship between theory and practice, particularly how theory informs practice, and/or how practice informs theory. Recent publications of note include: *Theory and Philosophy in Education Research: Methodological Dialogues* (Routledge), and *MacIntyre, Rationality and Education: Against Education of Our Age* (Springer).

**R. Scott Webster** is an Associate Professor, and the coordinator of the Curriculum, Pedagogy and Professional Learning group within the School of Education at Deakin University, Australia. His areas of research include philosophy and theories of education, teacher education, curriculum theory, existentialism, and spirituality. His authored and edited books include the following: *Educating for Meaningful Lives* (2009); *Understanding Curriculum: The Australian Context* (2019, 2nd ed., with A. Ryan); *Rethinking Reflection and Ethics for Teachers* (2019, with J. Whelan); and *Theory and Philosophy in Education Research: Methodological Dialogues* (2018).

## Educational Philosophy and Theory
*Series Editor: Peter Roberts, University of Canterbury, New Zealand*

This series is devoted to cutting-edge scholarship in educational philosophy and theory. Each book in the series focuses on a key theme or thinker and includes essays from a range of contributors. To be published in the series, a book will normally have first appeared as a special issue of *Educational Philosophy and Theory*, one of the premier philosophy of education journals in the world. This provides an assurance for readers of the quality of the work and enhances the visibility of the book in the international philosophy of education community. Books in this series combine creativity with rigour and insight. The series is intended to demonstrate the value of diverse theoretical perspectives in educational discourse, and contributors are invited to draw on literature, art and film as well as traditional philosophical sources in their work. Questions of educational policy and practice will also be addressed. The books published in this series will provide key reference points for subsequent theoretical work by other scholars, and will play a significant role in advancing philosophy of education as a field of study.

Recent titles in the series include:

**The Confucian Concept of Learning**
Revisited for East Asian Humanistic Pedagogies
*Edited by Duck-Joo Kwak, Morimichi Kato and Ruyu Hung*

**A Kaleidoscopic View of Chinese Philosophy of Education**
*Edited by Ruyu Hung*

**John Dewey's Democracy and Education in an Era of Globalization**
*Edited by Mordechai Gordon and Andrea R. English*

**Asian Perspectives on Education for Sustainable Development**
*Edited by Liz Jackson*

**Measuring Up in Education**
Philosophical Explorations for Justice and Democracy Within and Beyond Cultures of Measurement in Educational Systems
*Edited by Steven A. Stolz and R. Scott Webster*

**Cultivation of Self in East Asian Philosophy of Education**
*Edited by Ruyu Hung*

https://www.routledge.com/Educational-Philosophy-and-Theory/book-series/EPT

# Measuring Up in Education

Philosophical Explorations for Justice and Democracy Within and Beyond Cultures of Measurement in Educational Systems

*Edited by*
Steven A. Stolz and R. Scott Webster

LONDON AND NEW YORK

First published 2020
by Routledge
2 Park Square, Milton Park, Abingdon, Oxon, OX14 4RN

and by Routledge
52 Vanderbilt Avenue, New York, NY 10017

*Routledge is an imprint of the Taylor & Francis Group, an informa business*

© 2020 Philosophy of Education Society of Australasia

All rights reserved. No part of this book may be reprinted or reproduced or utilised in any form or by any electronic, mechanical, or other means, now known or hereafter invented, including photocopying and recording, or in any information storage or retrieval system, without permission in writing from the publishers.

*Trademark notice*: Product or corporate names may be trademarks or registered trademarks, and are used only for identification and explanation without intent to infringe.

*British Library Cataloguing-in-Publication Data*
A catalogue record for this book is available from the British Library

ISBN13: 978-0-367-36032-0

Typeset in ITC Galliard Std
by codeMantra

**Publisher's Note**
The publisher accepts responsibility for any inconsistencies that may have arisen during the conversion of this book from journal articles to book chapters, namely the inclusion of journal terminology.

**Disclaimer**
Every effort has been made to contact copyright holders for their permission to reprint material in this book. The publishers would be grateful to hear from any copyright holder who is not here acknowledged and will undertake to rectify any errors or omissions in future editions of this book.

# Contents

*Citation Information* vi
*Notes on Contributors* viii

Introduction: Measuring Up in Education 1
*Steven A. Stolz and R. Scott Webster*

1 Education, Measurement and the Professions: Reclaiming a space for democratic professionality in education 4
 *Gert Biesta*

2 Valuing and Desiring Purposes of Education to Transcend Miseducative Measurement Practices 20
 *R. Scott Webster*

3 Getting the Measure of Measurement: Global educational opportunity 36
 *Penny Enslin and Mary Tjiattas*

4 Creating the Civil Society East and West: Relationality, responsibility and the education of the humane person 51
 *Jānis (John) Tālivaldis Ozoliņš*

5 Can Educationally Significant Learning be Assessed? 68
 *Steven A. Stolz*

6 The Givenness of the Human Learning Experience and Its Incompatibility with Information Analytics 80
 *David Lundie*

7 A Quantum Measurement Paradigm for Educational Predicates: Implications for validity in educational measurement 94
 *Ian Cantley*

8 On the Un-becoming of Measurement in Education 111
 *Nuraan Davids*

*Index* 123

# Citation Information

The chapters in this book were originally published in *Educational Philosophy and Theory*, volume 49, issue 4 (April 2017). When citing this material, please use the original page numbering for each article, as follows:

**Introduction**
*Measuring Up in Education*
Steven A. Stolz and Scott Webster
*Educational Philosophy and Theory*, volume 49, issue 4 (April 2017) pp. 312–314

**Chapter 1**
*Education, Measurement and the Professions: Reclaiming a space for democratic professionality in education*
Gert Biesta
*Educational Philosophy and Theory*, volume 49, issue 4 (April 2017) pp. 315–330

**Chapter 2**
*Valuing and Desiring Purposes of Education to Transcend Miseducative Measurement Practices*
Robert Scott Webster
*Educational Philosophy and Theory*, volume 49, issue 4 (April 2017) pp. 331–346

**Chapter 3**
*Getting the Measure of Measurement: Global educational opportunity*
Penny Enslin and Mary Tjiattas
*Educational Philosophy and Theory*, volume 49, issue 4 (April 2017) pp. 347–361

**Chapter 4**
*Creating the Civil Society East and West: Relationality, responsibility and the education of the humane person*
Jānis (John) Tālivaldis Ozoliņš
*Educational Philosophy and Theory*, volume 49, issue 4 (April 2017) pp. 362–378

**Chapter 5**
*Can Educationally Significant Learning be Assessed?*
Steven A. Stolz
*Educational Philosophy and Theory*, volume 49, issue 4 (April 2017) pp. 379–390

## Chapter 6
*The Givenness of the Human Learning Experience and Its Incompatibility with Information Analytics*
David Lundie
*Educational Philosophy and Theory*, volume 49, issue 4 (April 2017) pp. 391–404

## Chapter 7
*A Quantum Measurement Paradigm for Educational Predicates: Implications for validity in educational measurement*
Ian Cantley
*Educational Philosophy and Theory*, volume 49, issue 4 (April 2017) pp. 405–421

## Chapter 8
*On the Un-becoming of Measurement in Education*
Nuraan Davids
*Educational Philosophy and Theory*, volume 49, issue 4 (April 2017) pp. 422–433

For any permission-related enquiries please visit:
http://www.tandfonline.com/page/help/permissions

# Contributors

**Gert Biesta** is a Professor of Public Education at the Centre for Public Education and Pedagogy at Maynooth University, Ireland; a Professorial Fellow in Educational Theory and Pedagogy at the Moray House School of Education at the University of Edinburgh, UK; and NIVOZ Professor for Education at the University of Humanistic Studies, Utrecht, the Netherlands. His work focuses on the theory of education and the theory, and philosophy of educational and social research, with a particular interest in relationships between education and democracy.

**Ian Cantley** is a Lecturer in Education (Mathematics) at Queen's University Belfast, UK. His research interests include the philosophy of education, the mathematical and philosophical foundations of educational measurement models, and mathematics education.

**Nuraan Davids** is a Lecturer in the Department of Education Policy in the Faculty of Education at Stellenbosch University, South Africa. Her interests include democratic citizenship education, Islamic education, and ethics in education, with a particular focus on educational policy, theory and practice, management, and leadership inquiry. She is an Associate Editor of the *South African Journal of Higher Education* and an Editorial Board Member of *Ethics and Education*.

**Penny Enslin** is a Professor and Chair of Education at the University of Glasgow, UK, and Professor Emeritus in the School of Education at the University of the Witwatersrand, Johannesburg, South Africa. Her research interests and publications are in political philosophy and education with particular reference to democratic citizenship, cosmopolitan justice, and gender in education.

**David Lundie** is a Senior Lecturer in Education at Liverpool Hope University, UK. His research interests include digital ethics, educational technology, and religious and moral education. He is a member of the International Network Observatory on Big Data and the Professional Forum for Philosophy of Educational Technology.

**Jānis (John) Tālivaldis Ozoliņš** is a Professor of Philosophy at the Australian Catholic University, Brisbane, Australia, and Honorary Fellow at the Institute of Philosophy and Sociology at the University of Latvia, Riga, Latvia. He is a foreign member of the Latvian Academy of Sciences. He is a Fellow of the Higher Education Research and Development Society of Australasia, and a Fellow and the former President of the Philosophy of Education Society of Australasia. His philosophical interests include the metaphysics and moral philosophy of Aquinas, classical Confucian philosophy, applied ethics, and philosophy of education.

**Steven A. Stolz, PhD**, is a Senior Lecturer at La Trobe University, Australia. He has a diverse array of research interests, which ranges from: critical theory, epistemology, phenomenology, embodied cognition, narrative inquiry, and learning theories in psychology. At the moment, his primary area of scholarship is concerned with the relationship between theory and practice, particularly how theory informs practice, and/or how practice informs theory. Recent publications of note include: *Theory and Philosophy in Education Research: Methodological Dialogues* (Routledge), and *MacIntyre, Rationality and Education: Against Education of Our Age* (Springer).

**Mary Tjiattas** is a Teaching Assistant Professor, who teaches applied ethics, at North Carolina State University, Raleigh, USA. Her research interests are in social and political philosophy, moral psychology, and philosophy of social science and psychoanalysis.

**R. Scott Webster** is an Associate Professor, and the coordinator of the Curriculum, Pedagogy and Professional Learning group within the School of Education at Deakin University, Australia. His areas of research include philosophy and theories of education, teacher education, curriculum theory, existentialism, and spirituality.

# INTRODUCTION
# Measuring Up in Education

STEVEN A. STOLZ AND R. SCOTT WEBSTER

When we think about the notion of "measurement", there is a tendency to see closed and therefore quantifiable systems that act in producing a reductive concept of X enabling its measurement, which in turn can be used to compare X against Y, X against Z and so on, *ad infinitum*. Indeed, we often overlook the fact that the concept of measurement is a man-made construct essentially used to assign a quantity to an object and/or event based on predefined values. Take for instance the International System of Units (commonly known as "SI" which is an abbreviation taken from the French language name of "Système International d'Unités") used as a system of measurement in the sciences such as the metre. In the case of the metre—which was established by the Metre Convention in the late nineteenth century—we can see clear attempts to both reach universal consensus surrounding the act of measuring a metre and a sophisticated system of oversight used to maintain established conventions and standards such as expert committees. Certainly, our valuing of and reference to quantifiable systems such as the act of measuring a metre is no accident, particularly the notion of maintaining standards. A precursory survey of contemporary educational systems brings to our attention the ubiquitous place of assessment. Although most would agree that assessment has an important role to play in schooling, the concern we have at the moment revolves around a noticeable trend in education that seems to be preoccupied with measuring a range of educational events as if they were valuable in and of themselves, such as teacher/lecturer effectiveness, research quality, school/university league tables or rankings, ongoing large-scale public testing of students' progress in certain predefined areas captured at different reference points in their schooling and so on to name a few examples, which have all come to replace concerns about "education" itself and the improvement of the quality of life in a general sense. In a sense, measurement and educational assessment share a close relationship. Undeniably, we couldn't have the latter without the former; however, the idea that assessment is infallible because it claims to utilise objective means of measuring X, Y and Z or can compare X against Y, X against Z and so on is problematic on a number of different levels. Clearly, not all student learning that occurs in the name of education can be neatly measured in the same way as a metre. Likewise, teacher/lecturer effectiveness cannot—nor should be—be judged according to the results obtained by the students being taught. Although we have only briefly touched on some of the issues confronting contemporary schooling and educational systems that relate to the close relationship between measurement and assessment, the seven essays found within this *Educational Philosophy and Theory* special issue titled "Measuring Up in Education" is based on the 2013 Philosophy of Education Society of Australasia (PESA) conference theme that was held at the University of Melbourne from the 6$^{th}$ to 9th of December 2013. Each paper found within this special issue picks-up on this theme in various forms and contributes to the ongoing debate surrounding the role of measurement and assessment in education.

The first paper by Biesta focuses upon the democratic dimensions of the profession of being an educator and argues that practices in this current "age/culture of measurement" actually "distort" the democratic dimension, both for the profession and as a consequence, for democracy in society more generally. To help frame his argument, he draws upon the notion of normative validity to bring to the fore what ought to be of most importance in our understanding of the purposes of education, and what makes practices in this field "good" and hence possibly worthy of being measured.

This re-connection with end purposes of education that educators ought to have is taken up in the second paper by Webster who uses Dewey's notion of an end-in-view to argue that educators must come to *desire* end-purposes to transcend fragmentary and reductive tendencies typical of this age of measurement.

The third paper by Enslin and Tjiattas also calls for educative and societal practices to transcend the reductive practices of measurement which narrows our understanding of social justice. They draw upon Sen and Nussbaum's notion of capabilities to both challenge and re-imagine how social justice might be pursued by challenging the assumed aggregative nature of some measurements to enable more authentic voices to participate in how we might all understand justice and what are considered to be "good" measures of it.

Concern with social justice is continued in the fourth paper by Ozolins who explores the notion of a civil society by drawing upon ideas from both East and West. He largely employs the works of Gramsci and Confucianism to explore how the humanising aspects of society must not be lost via narrow understandings of measurement practices and that our fulfilment as human individuals and as members of a society can only be realised through relationships, and this must be included when measurements are used to make judgements.

The fifth paper by Stolz explores whether the most valuable sort of learning associated with education actually lends themselves to being assessed. He challenges the excessive hegemonic practices of the current culture of assessment. This in-turn leads to a re-evaluation of what might count as valuable sorts of knowledge in education. Likewise, Lundie picks up on this theme of hegemonic assessment practices, and argues that the proliferation of "Big Data" in education raises a number of questions about the nature of what is measurable, particularly in relation to the assumptions underpinning learning analytics. Lundie demonstrates this by drawing upon Descartes and Marion to make the case that the learner must be understood as an intentional and self-knowing subject rather than be reduced to an information depository/processor, and as such this nature is non-informational. Finally, the seventh paper by Cantley makes the case that many of the problems with current measurement practices exist due to the dominance of a Newtonian framework, and argues that measurement may be more meaningful if understood through a quantum perspective.

Drawing upon Bohr and Wittgenstein, he makes the case for context-specific measurements rather than universal, high-stakes approaches, in order to better represent educational achievements.

In summary, the close relationship between measurement, assessment and evaluation is so dominant, and yet hidden that we sometimes fail to see and appreciate it fully in any meaningful way. Consequently, we are now witnessing the dehumanising effects on the lives of some individuals and communities because the objectified tendencies of assessment and measurement are not being recognised or challenged in a sustained or rigorous manner. These seven essays uncover and remind us of the inescapable relationship between measurement and assessment in educational systems, and challenge us to rethink measurement and how we use it in our educational practice or practices.

# Education, Measurement and the Professions: Reclaiming a space for democratic professionality in education

GERT BIESTA

**Abstract**

*In this article, I explore the impact of the contemporary culture of measurement on education as a professional field. I focus particularly on the democratic dimensions of professionalism, which includes both the democratic qualities of professional action in education itself and the way in which education, as a profession, supports the wider democratic cause. I show how an initial authoritarian conception of professionalism was opened up in the 1960s and 1970s towards more democratic and more inclusive forms of professional action. I then show how, in the wake of the transformation of the welfare state and the rise of neo-liberal forms of governing, the democratic dimension of professionalism became distorted. I discuss three distortions: having to do with the position of clients, the nature of accountability and the status of professional knowledge. While at first sight, the developments in each of these areas can be seen as furthering the democratisation of the professions, I argue that in fact they have eroded the democratic dimension of the professions and show the contribution of the culture of measurement to this erosion process. In the final step of my argument, I suggest how a more democratic mode of professional action might be regained and how such a mode of professional action might contribute to wider processes of democratisation.*

**Introduction: Education in an Age of Measurement**

Oscar Wilde's famous contention that nowadays people know the price of everything but the value of nothing—which is offered as a definition of a cynic—seems to capture quite well one of the main problems of the 'age of measurement' (Biesta, 2009a, 2010a) in which contemporary education appears to operate. We live in a time, after all, in which there is an abundance of information about the performance of individual students, groups of students, schools, school districts and even of national educational systems as a whole, just as the global measurement industry is trying to pin down the exact 'value' teachers are supposedly adding to all this. But while the performance of many aspects of the education system is measured in much detail and with much precision and statistical sophistication, the question that remains is whether this brings us any closer to an understanding of the value of the processes and practices that are being measured. The question that remains, in other words, is whether what is going on in our age of measurement is getting us any closer to an understanding of what makes education *good*, rather than what makes it merely effective or efficient.

This is not just a matter of the *technical validity* of the measurements being conducted, which concerns the question whether such measurements are measuring what they are supposed to measure. There is the additional and much more urgent question of what I have elsewhere suggested to call the *normative validity* of such measurements (Biesta, 2010a). This concerns the question whether what is being measured actually represents what we value about education, that is whether it corresponds to our conception of good education. It is here that we can find one of the major problems of the current measurement regime in education. Simply put it is the question whether we are measuring what we value, or whether we are valuing what is being measured. We might think of this as an open question, but perhaps it is more accurate to treat it as a diagnosis of what is currently going on in many countries around the world, where we have reached a situation where measurement is to a large degree driving education policy and practice without any longer asking whether what is being measured adequately represents a view of good education. One example of this can be found in what is known as 'performativity' (see Ball, 2003; Lyotard, 1984). This is the situation where *indicators* of quality are taken as *definitions* of quality. We can see this happening, for example, when reaching a certain position in a league table becomes itself a strategic target for an organisation.

The impact of the measurement regime on contemporary education is at least partly the result of its sheer size—which is why I find it appropriate to speak of a global measurement *industry*. But while size matters, it is also important to note the way in which the measurement industry has managed to bring a wide range of actors with significantly different interests into one network, including researchers, academics, national governments, commercial publishers and supra-national organisations such as the OECD and the World Bank, thus creating, as Latour (1987) has called it, a strong *asymmetry* between those who are inside the network and who are outside of it. This makes it significantly more difficult, more expensive, and more energy- and time-consuming to interrupt and oppose this network with meaningful alternatives, even to the point where the impression may arrive that 'there is no alternative'.

There are two further dimensions that matter here: one having to do with the rhetorical dimensions of the discussion and the other with its social psychology. With regard to the first, it is important to note that the culture of measurement stems from a complex rationale which combines a number of different discourses and agendas, connected to such notions as accountability, control, transparency, evidence, choice and social justice. The problem at a rhetorical level is that this allows for a 'quick switch' (Charlton, 2002) between the different discourses, which makes it more difficult to effectively challenge and criticise the modes of functioning of the measurement regime. Think, for example of the way in which a critique of measurement as a form of teacher control is rebuffed by playing the social justice argument that transparency is needed in order to make sure that everyone has access to good education. Given that different discourses, agendas and interests are at stake, the problem that quickly arises is that it is not clear which ends are supposed to justify which means—or to put it more cynically: it is precisely because of this confused connection between means and ends that people can get away with more than that they should be able to get away with.

With regard to the social psychology of the measurement regime, the question remains why people are attracted to it or, put differently, why so many people fall for it. Fear plays an important role here. There is first of all the pseudo-security of numbers, stemming from the idea that measurements are objective and can release us from the more difficult task of making judgements. That this security is a pseudo-security is because measurement is ultimately about expressing one thing in terms of another, so that the underlying standard is basically arbitrary, and always turns us back to judgement. The measurement industry is also fuelled by a fear of risk and a concomitant desire for control. Here, we should not forget that if we try to control education completely, we turn it into a machinery in which what matters educationally—such as the freedom and independence of the student—is ultimately squeezed out (on this, see Biesta, 2014). And perhaps the most important driver of the measurement industry is the fear of being left behind. This is the fear that other countries or education systems will, in some respect or on some criterion, do better than we do. The problem here is that one often forgets to ask whether one really would like to be the same as those one is lagging behind to and what the status is of the criteria on which some are positioned as being more 'ahead' than others. Should we indeed simply accept that with regard to its education system every country wants to become like Finland, Singapore or South Korea?

In this article I wish to focus on one particular aspect of the culture of measurement, which is the way in which it is impacting on professional fields such as education. I am particularly interested in the impact on the democratic dimensions of professionalism. This includes both the democratic dimensions of professions themselves—and I will say more about this below—and the way in which professions 'serve' the wider democratic cause. I will first show how an initial authoritarian conception of professionalism was 'opened up' in the 1960s and 1970s towards more democratic and more inclusive forms of professional action. I will then show how, in the wake of the transformation of the welfare state and the rise of neo-liberal forms of governing, the democratic dimension of professionalism became distorted. I discuss three distortions, having to do with the position of clients, the nature of accountability, and the status of professional knowledge. While at first sight, the developments in each of these areas can be seen as furthering the democratisation of the professions, I will argue that in fact they have eroded the democratic dimension of the professions. I will also show that the culture of measurement has played and is continuing to play an important role in this.

In the final step of my argument, I suggest how a more democratic mode of professional action might be regained and how such a mode of professional action might actually contribute to wider processes of democratisation.

The particular approach that I pursue in this contribution might perhaps best be characterised as normative in that I explore a particular *idea* and *ideal* of the professions rather than that I give a sociological analysis of the actual operation of those who refer to themselves as professionals (a classic example of the latter kind is Sarfatti Larson, 1979).

## The Democratisation of the Professions

The traditional case for professional autonomy, that is for the idea that professionals should regulate and control their own work, relies on three assumptions (see, e.g. Carr, 2000; Freidson, 1994). The first is that the work of professionals distinguishes itself from many other areas of work in that it is concerned with the promotion of *human well-being*. This already indicates that professionality is not merely technical but always entails a normative dimension. Secondly, it is argued that unlike many other fields of work, professional work relies on *highly specialist knowledge and skills*, which is one of the reasons why the education of the traditional professions (doctors, lawyers and priests) has always taken place in institutions of higher education. Thirdly, it is argued that the work of professionals distinguishes itself from other areas of work because professionals work in *relationships of authority and trust*. These three assumptions constitute, on the one hand, a *definition* of professionalism and therefore appear each time a new area of work seeks to elevate itself to the status of a profession. On the other hand, the assumptions constitute a *justification* for the special status of the professions and for its system of self-regulation.

The traditional configuration of professionalism sees professions as closed and largely inward-looking entities that, although performing important functions for society, in a sense operate at a distance and even isolated from society. In their traditional set-up, professions thus largely operate beyond democratic control, either from clients or from society at large. This is most clearly visible in the fact that professions regulate their own functioning with regard to quality control, entrance to the profession—including the regulation of professional education—and, in case of professional failure and misconduct, also the 'exit' from the profession. This makes professions into powerful entities that exert power both over their own functioning and over important domains of human well-being. The power of professions also helps to understand why relations of authority and trust can easily turn into unjustified exertion of power and even abuse of power.

The democratic deficit of the professions was fundamentally exposed and challenged in the 1960s and 1970s, partly as a result of client and patient emancipation (e.g. in the medical domain and psychiatry), and partly as a result of changing conceptions of health and mental well-being, for example in alternative medicine and anti-psychiatry (such as the work of R. D. Laing; see, e.g. Laing, 1960; Laing & Esterson, 1964; for medicine see also Hellín, 2002). These developments, which themselves were part of wider protest and emancipation movements at the time (including the student revolts of 1968 and the rise of the anti-education movement in Germany, known as *anti-Pädagogik*; see, e.g. von Braunmühl, 1975), particularly exposed the abuse of power within professional relationships and, through this, were aimed at what we might call a democratic redefinition of the relationship between professionals and their clients. To the extent to which, after the Second World War, many professions became more central in the project of the welfare state (see, e.g. Björkman, 1982), a further shift occurred from a strict orientation on individual clients and their needs towards a wider concern for the common good. This can be seen as a second democratising impulse where professions increasingly established relationships of democratic accountability with their clients and society more generally.

## Three Post-democratic Distortions

This potted history of the development of professions and professionalism is first of all important in order to make visible how in the 1960s and 1970s a democratisation of the traditional configuration of the professions was set into motion, both as a result of a redefinition of the relationship between professionals and their clients, and as a result of the redefinition of the relationship between professions and professionals and their societal environment—something that was particularly connected to the role of the professions in emerging welfare states after the Second World War. Understanding these developments is also important, however, in order to grasp the significance of more recent shifts and changes in professional fields such as health care and education which, at first sight, may appear as furthering the case for the democratisation of professions but which, on closer inspection, turn out to be undermining the democratic configuration of professional work. In this section, I focus on three 'post-democratic distortions': (1) the transformation of clients, patients and also students into customers; (2) the transformation of a democratic conception of accountability into a technical-managerial conception; and (3) the transformation of professional knowledge into 'evidence', linked to the idea of evidence-based practice.

These developments should be understood against the background of the transformation of the welfare state and the rise of neo-liberal forms of governance and governing. The transformation of the welfare state—which was partly the result of economic crises such as the oil crisis in the 1970s, and partly of ideological interventions such as the conservative idea of the small state ('Thatcherism') (see Faulks, 1998)—resulted in a shift from an orientations towards social justice and solidarity (the idea of 'the common good') towards a view of the state as a provider of a limited set of public services. What neo-liberalism added to this was the redefinition of the state as a regulator of the market of public services, no longer concerned with a substantive and hence political definition of the common good, but with formal notions such as 'quality', 'choice' and 'the customer always comes first'. As a result, neo-liberal governments no longer see themselves as a key actor in the political debate about the definition of the common good, but increasingly understand themselves as process managers who, through a regime of standards, measurement and inspection, try to secure the quality of the products on offer. 'Quality' itself is understood in strictly formal terms, that is as the situation where a particular provision or service meets certain standards, without—as I have already hinted at in the introduction to this article—any concern for the question how meaningful those standards actually are. In what way, then, have professional fields been caught up in these developments and how has this distorted their democratic potential?

*A First Distortion: From Client/Patient/Student to Customer*

I have indicated above that the emancipation of clients, patients and students in the 1960s and 1970s not only exposed the democratic deficit of many professions but also resulted in a transformation of professions and, more specifically, a transformation of professional relationships. Clients, patients and students literally made their voices heard in order to make clear that they were not just objects of the action and interventions of professionals, but subjects in their own right who therefore wanted to be treated as subjects of dialogue and not objects of intervention. From this angle, it may seem that the recent trend to refer to clients, patients and students as customers, and the tendency to emphasise that in such domains as health care and education professionals must offer what their customers want, is the ultimate step in the democratisation of the professions—one where those at the receiving end, so to speak, are in total control.

But is this indeed the ultimate step in the democratisation of the professions? I have reasons to doubt that this is the case, and the main reason has to do with a fundamental difference between economic transactions and professional transactions (see Feinberg, 2001). Whereas in economic transactions, customers know what they want and would just look for a company that can provide them with what they want for the best possible combination of price and quality, a key aspect of professional relationships is that professional not just service the needs of their 'clients' but also play a key role in the definition of what it is that their clients need. Clients, patients and students, in other words, do not engage with professionals just to get what they already know that they want. Part of the process is precisely to figure what it is that clients actually need. As Feinberg (2001) explains: we go to the doctor because we have a headache, but we expect that the doctor figures out what the headache is an indication of and what can be done to get rid of it. This already suggested that the redefinition of clients, patients and students as customers is based on a fundamental misunderstanding of what professional practices are and what they are about.

A clear example of what is at stake here can be found in the domain of education and upbringing. If parents were only to give their children what they say they want, and never raise the question—for themselves but also in dialogue with their children—whether what their children say they want is actually good for them, it is quite likely that their children will turn into spoilt brats who remain slaves of their desires rather than that they are in a position where they can have a mature perspective on their desires in order to judge which of their desires are actually desirable. It is here that we can locate the specific responsibility of educators, and a similar argument can be made in relation to most if not all professions: just giving clients what they say they want may be utterly unprofessional. Doctors are not just there to give their patients just what they want, but have a key role in finding out what might be wrong with the patient in order then to propose possible treatments. Patients do have a voice in all this—for example with regard to questions concerning the risks and benefits of a certain treatment—but this is always to be understood as a *dialogue* between the experiential expertise of the patient and the professional expertise of the doctor. It is not a process where the doctor simply sells what the patient wants to have.

For precisely these reasons then, the redefinition of clients, patients and students as customers is not a further step in the democratisation of professional work and professional relationships, but rather a development that subverts the unique contribution professionals make. The reason for this lies in the fact that the redefinition of clients, patients and students as customers only puts the authoritarian relationship on its head by giving all the power to the customer. What it fails to see is that real emancipation and real democratisation requires a *redefinition* of the relationship between professionals and their clients where both play a distinctive role in a dialogical process of needs definition—it is not just a *reversal* of the traditional set-up that would make the client/customer powerful and the professional powerless.

*A Second Distortion: From Democratic to Technical-managerial Accountability*

A second distortion has to do with the way in which a democratic conception of accountability has been replaced by a technical-managerial one (on this see also Biesta, 2004). In a democratic conception of accountability, professionals are accountable for the quality of their professional action in a direct dialogical relationship with their stakeholders (clients, patients, students and ultimately society as a whole). In a technical-managerial conception of accountability, however, the focus is no longer on the quality of professional action. Rather professionals are held accountable for the degree in which their actions meet certain standards. The role of the state in this set-up, as already alluded to, is to guarantee the quality of the 'product' delivered by the professions. But it does not do so by engaging in a substantial political discussion about what, for example good mental health care or good education ought to be, but by formulating standards and by initiating systems of inspection and control that need to make sure that professionals services meet the standards. The question of the normative validity of the standards is hardly ever discussed, or is brushed aside as 'ideological'. What happens as a result of this is the creation of a gap between professionals (redefined as providers) and their clients (redefined as customers). In this gap, we find a whole machinery of often privatised quality controllers and inspectors, which means that the accountability relationships between professionals and their clients are no longer direct but have become indirect.

This is another example of what, at first sight, seems to further the democratisation of the professions but what, on closer inspection, turns out to be an erosion of the possibility for substantial democratic dialogue between professions/professionals and their clients. In her Reith lectures on accountability, Onara O'Neill (O'Neill, 2002) has shown in much detail what goes wrong here. She reveals two important shifts in the rise of the technical-managerial approach to accountability. The first has to do with a shift with regard to the different parties involved in accountability processes. She writes:

> In theory the new culture of accountability and audit makes professionals and institutions more accountable to the public. This is supposedly done by publishing targets and levels of attainment in league tables, and by establishing complaint procedures by which members of the public can seek redress for any professional or institutional failures. But underlying this ostensible aim of accountability to the public the real requirements are for accountability to regulators, to departments of government, to funders, to legal standards. The new forms of accountability impose forms of central control—quite often indeed a range of different and mutually inconsistent forms of central control. (O'Neill, 2002)

A second shift has to do with definitions of quality. Here she writes:

> In theory again the new culture of accountability and audit makes professionals and institutions more accountable *for good performance*. This is manifest in the rhetoric of improvement and raising standards, of efficiency gains and best practice, of respect for patients and pupils and employees. But beneath this admirable rhetoric the real focus is on performance indicators chosen for ease of measurement and control rather than because they measure accurately what the quality of performance is. (O'Neill, 2002)

O'Neill's observations thus clearly show the difference between a democratic and a technical-managerial approach to accountability and the slippery slope between the two.

*A Third Distortion: From Professional Knowledge to Evidence-based Practice*

The third arena in which the democratisation of professionalism has been distorted has to do with the way in which professional judgement in a range of different professional domains is increasingly being replaced or pushed out by a demand for an evidence-based approach (for more detail see Biesta, 2007, 2010b). The idea here is that professional action can only become really professional if it is no longer based on the singular insights (or according to some subjective opinions) of professionals, but when it becomes based upon secure scientific knowledge about 'what works'. And the claim is that the *only* way in which we can be certain that a professional intervention 'works' is by means of randomised controlled trials—in the literature known as 'golden standard'—which has even led to situations where professionals are prevented from doing anything unless there is positive evidence that their interventions will work.

While proponents of evidence-based approaches claim that professional fields such as education, social work and care can be improved dramatically if they opt for the evidence-based approach which, so it is claimed, has been the main driver of progress in such fields as agriculture and medicine (see for this particular argument Slavin, 2002), there are a number of reasons why the idea of 'what works' is actually not that easily incorporated. One key issue is that in domains such as care and education—although this ultimately also holds for agriculture and medicine—the question can never simply be about 'what works' but always needs to be phrases as the question 'What works for what?' The point is that any idea of 'working' always needs to be understood in relation to the aim or aims of professional action in a particular field. This already shows that the question of 'what works' can, at most, be relevant with regard to the means of professional action, but not with regard to the ends.

The more important point with regard to the question whether the idea of an evidence-based approach makes sense in domains of professional action has to do with the fact that all professional action takes place in what Aristotle already distinguished as the domain of the 'variable' (see Aristotle, 1980), the domain of actions and possible consequences, and not in the domain of the 'eternal', that is the domain of cause-effect relationships. One reason for this lies in the fact that professional action takes place between human beings who never appear just as objects of intervention—which also shows that the language of intervention is actually quite misleading—but always also as subjects in their own right. In the domain of the variable, research can at most provide us with information about *possible* relationships between actions and consequences. But research can never guarantee that relationships between actions and consequences that were found in the past will appear in exactly the same way in the present. While research therefore can tell us what in a concrete situation and under specific circumstances *has worked* in the past, it can never tell us what *will work* in the present or the future. Next to the need to make judgements about the ends of professional action, we therefore also always need judgement about how to act—which is a judgement about the application of general and decontextualised knowledge to concrete situations and singular cases. Scientific evidence can neither replace judgements about how to act, nor can it replace judgements about the aims and ends of professional action—and where we find claims that it can or should, we have an example of positivism, where the means are defining the ends, rather than that we are in a position to define the ends of our actions ourselves.

The call, and in some cases even the blunt demand to work in an evidence-based way thus appears as an attempt to eradicate professional judgement with regard to the 'how' and the 'what for' of professional action from the domain of professionalism. It seeks to transform professions into abstract 'machines' in which reflection and judgement are seen as a weakness rather than as an essential part. This shows how the call for an evidence-based approach is not a deepening of the knowledge and judgement of professionals, but rather an attempt to overrule such knowledge and judgement. In precisely this sense, the evidence-based approach is another erosion of the democratic dimension of professionalism and hence another post-democratic distortion.

**The Role of Measurement**

If the above provides us with an insight into the ways in which recent developments in professional fields such as education are hindering rather than enhancing their democratic potential, there is the additional question how the culture of measurement is contributing to this. With regard to this question, I wish to make two observations. Firstly, I wish to argue that with regard to each distortion there is a need for data, information and measurement. After all, to give customers what they want and to give the choice and value for money they need data about the quality of the products on offer. Also to hold professionals accountable for the quality of their performance, we need data about the degree to which their work meets preset standards. And in order to make professional activity evidence-based, there is a need for data about what works, particularly data that show correlations (if not causal connections) between 'interventions' and 'outcomes'.

We can say, therefore, that the culture of measurement has played and continues to play a key role in the post-democratic transformation of the professions. But it is not only that the transformations *require* data and measurement. At the very same time, the availability of data, information and measurement *reinforce* these particular distortions rather than that they work against them. After all, once there are data available about the performance of individuals, groups or systems, it becomes increasingly difficult not to look at the data. Similarly, once there are data about the performance of individuals, groups or systems, it is difficult not to include them in any accountability exercise. And once some kind of apparent 'evidence' has been constructed about particular practices and ways of working, it becomes again difficult not to make use of it. The availability of data, information and measurement, to put it differently, is seductive and difficult to resist—which reveals another dimension of the social psychology of the culture of measurement and provides a further explanation for its attractiveness and 'force'. What then are the options for 'fighting back' and reclaiming a democratic space for professionalism—which can also be understood as reclaiming a space for the democratic professional, that is the professional who sees it as his or her fundamental professional responsibility to work in a democratic rather than an authoritarian way? I wish to make three suggestions.

## Reclaiming a Space for Democratic Professionalism

The first thing that needs to be done—to which I have contributed in this article—is to challenge, interrupt and resist the redefinition of the professions, particular with regard to the three distortions I have analysed above: the redefinition of the client/patient/student as a customer; the replacement of democratic accountability with technical-managerial accountability; and the attempt to replace professional knowledge with evidence about 'what works'. In each case, it is particularly important to show that these developments are based on a misunderstanding of what professional work is about—for which I have provided arguments in the foregoing as well.

Secondly, it is important to expose the democratic deficit of these developments, that is to show that in spite of what may seem to be the case at first sight, they are actually undermining and eroding the development of more democratic ways of working in professional fields such as health care and education. For this, it is important to highlight—as I have done—that democratisation of the professions is not a matter of reversing the positions of the involved parties, that is just turning authoritarian relationships on their head. It rather requires the establishment of new relationships between professionals and their clients—relationships of dialogue where both can contribute their particular experience and expertise, acknowledging that the experience and expertise of each of the parties involved (professionals and clients) is different and complementary, and that the differing contributions from all are needed in order transform authoritarian into democratic professional relationships.

To resist post-democratic transformations of dimensions of professional work, and to insist on the need to transform relationships rather than just reverse them, often means that one finds oneself defending ideas and positions that, at first sight, may look outdated. For example, to argue against the 'learnification' of education (Biesta, 2010a), that is against a conception of education that puts the learner at the centre and sidelines the teacher, and, in response, to make a case for the importance of teaching and the teacher (Biesta, 2012) is often perceived as a step back rather than a step forward. So it needs careful argumentation to show that the turn towards the learner and away from the teacher is actually in inadequate response to authoritarian forms of teaching as control, as it only reverses the position of the student and teacher, rather than that it seeks to transform the nature of their relationship. Similarly, to argue that education should be understood as value-based rather than evidence-based (Biesta, 2010b) is often perceived as a return to a pre-scientific age rather than as an attempt to show that science—in the form of evidence or otherwise—can never do away with the need for judgement in education.

The overarching task in all this is to resist technicist conceptions of professionalism, such as the reduction of the role of the teacher to that of a technician who just implements and executes pre-specified routines (see also Leaton Gray, 2007), and to provide a viable and robust alternative. Throughout this article, such a different conception of professionalism has been emerging. In the final section, I wish to highlight the key dimensions of this conception of professionalism, taking my examples from teaching. I will also show how this conception of professionalism connects to the question of democracy, thus outlining a conception of the democratic professional and democratic professionalism.

**Conceptualising the Democratic Professional**

I wish to suggest that professional work is characterised by three aspects: (1) an orientation towards the 'telos' of the practice; (2) engagement with processes of needs definition; and (3) engagement with the transformation of power into authority. Let me clarify what I have in mind.

I started this article with the traditional definition of professionality. There I argued that professions are characterised by an orientation towards human well-being. This already reveals that professional action is never merely technical, that is it is never just concerned with the production of a particular effect or a particular outcome, but rather is orientated towards the realisation of the 'telos' of the particular practice. Although we might translate the Greek word 'telos' with 'aim', it is more appropriate to translate it with 'purpose', as the 'telos' of a practice refers to that which the practice seeks to promote in a more general sense. In health care, the 'telos' is the promotion of health; in the legal professions, it is the promotion of justice; whereas in education, we might say that it is the promotion of 'educatedness', which, for example can be characterised as the promotion of the cognitive and moral independence of students.

Whereas the aims of professional action are the more concrete achievements or results professionals seek to bring about, the purpose or 'telos' of a practice refers to that which gives a practice its meaning, identity and sense of direction. This is why it is a mistake to think of teaching, for example simply as the production of measurable 'learning outcomes'. While there may be a place for this in teaching, it can never be the be all and end all of education but need to be considered in relation to the wider 'telos' of education. The question as to what the 'telos' of education should be, is a question that cannot simply be settled once and for all, but rather requires ongoing reflection and deliberation amongst interested parties, for example with regard to the criteria of what would count as an educated person. Answering this question is never a matter of facts, but always involves normative preferences and choices. This already is one important reason why teaching, just as all other professions that are constituted by a 'telos', has to be understood as a normative profession, not just a technical one (on the idea of normative professionalism see Kunneman, 1996).

The second characteristic of the conception of professionalism I am putting forward in this article concerns the fact that professionals do not simply service the needs of their clients, but play a key role in defining those needs. Whereas in the traditional conception of professionality, this was seen as the sole responsibility of the professional—the idea of 'doctor knows best'—in democratic conceptions of professionality; this is understood as a dialogical process in which professionals and their clients both have something to contribute. It is important to bear in mind that professionals and their clients occupy different roles and carry different responsibilities in this relationship.

In education, the process of needs definition takes the form of introducing a distinction between what children and students desire and what can considered to be desirable for them—both with regard to their individual lives and the lives they live with others. This is for example how the French educationalist Meirieu (2008) characterises the core 'interest' of education, namely as a process where we try to release children from their desires by opening up a distinction between what they desire and what might be desirable for them. In the first instance, educators play a central role in answering this question for the children and students they are responsible for. But over time this question—'Is what I desire also desirable for me?'—should become a question children and students ask about their own desires. At that point, one could say that they have developed a mature perspective on their desires and are no longer dominated by them. This suggests that educational processes are not merely affirmative in that they do not simply accept the desires of children and students, but always entail moments of interruption where such desires are examined and questioned (see Biesta, 2009b). To initiate such interruptions, to ask students which of their desires are actually desirable for them, is again not a factual matter but a thoroughly normative endeavour that requires judgements about which desires are to be valued.

The third aspect of the conception of professionality I am putting forward in this article has to do with the fact that professional relationships are characterised by the presence of authority. It is very important here to make a distinction between power and authority, and hence between authoritarian relationships and relationships of authority. Whereas authoritarian relationships are about one-sided power and control, relationships of authority are relationships of what we might call 'accepted' or 'justified' power. This first of all highlights that authority is fundamentally relational (see Bingham, 2008). It is not something one person can possess and can exercise over another person, but has to be understood as something that 'circulates' in relationships and thus requires 'support' from all parties in the relationship. It is not, for example that teachers automatically have authority over their students, but they can, in the development of their mutual relationships, be given authority by their students —they can be 'authorised' by their students, so to speak. The transformation of (relationships of) power into (relationships of) authority is one of the key dynamics of all professional relationships if they seek to operate in a democratic rather than an authoritarian way.

To think of professions in terms of their 'telos', in terms of needs definition and in terms of the transformation of power into authority, outlines a notion of professionality that is quite different from the direction in which the current culture of measurements seeks to steer professional fields such as education. Moreover, to think of these dimensions in dialogical rather than one-sided terms highlights the way in which professions can operate democratically rather than that they become dominated by the quasi-democracy of markets, customers and standards. What is interesting about this way of understanding what democratic professionality is about, is that the aspects of 'telos', needs definition and authority can actually also be seen as defining characteristics of democracy itself.

As I have argued elsewhere in more detail (see, e.g. Biesta, 2013), democracy is not to be understood as something 'natural' but rather as a historical intervention, that is a way of conducting our collective lives based on a commitment to a set of specific values, namely those of equality, liberty and solidarity. As Chantal Mouffe has argued, these values constitute the democratic sphere, albeit that the interpretation of what these values actually stands for has to be ongoing (see Mouffe, 2000). This suggests that (the practice of) democracy is itself constituted by a 'telos' that gives it distinctiveness and meaning. A second important point is that, unlike what many seem to think, democracy is not about choice. It is not about the simple expression of one's preferences and the counting of preferences in order then to give all power to the majority. Democracy is rather to be understood as a process in which the 'wants' and desires of individuals are brought into collective deliberation in order to figure which of those wants and desires can legitimately be 'carried' by the collective. This is far from an arithmetical process, but a truly transformative and also truly educative one, which actually can be understood as a process of collective needs definition. One could say that the outcome of such processes of deliberation establish what should have authority in our collective lives. In this regard, we can say that democracy itself is characterised by the transformation of power into authority.

Looking at democracy in this way reveals a structural resemblance between the ways in which the democratic professional works and the way in which democracy itself operates, which suggests that the democratisation of the professions along these lines is not only relevant for the 'internal' democratic quality of professional fields but also provides important opportunities for practising and experiencing the wider dynamics of democracy. In this regard, democratic professions perform an important contribution to wider processes of societal democratisation.

## Concluding Remarks

In this article, I have explored the impact of the culture of measurement on professional fields such as education. I have done this through an analysis of the transformation of professions in light of the decline of the welfare state and the rise of neo-liberal forms of governing and governance. I have shown that measurement plays an important role in these transformations—transformations that seek to push professions into the direction of standards-driven, evidence-based service providers. Whereas at first sight, the transparency and accountability and customer orientation that comes with this reconfiguration of the professions may look like a further democratisation of the professions, I have shown that these developments actually imply an erosion of their democratic potential. It is against this background that I have outlined the contours of a different conception of professionality in which an orientation towards the 'telos' of the profession and an engagement with needs definition and the transformation of power relations into relationships of authority are central. Such a democratic conception of professionality provides a starting point for reclaiming what professions such as education operating in a democratic society ought to be about. It provides a starting point, in other words, for a robust and reasoned response against the current erosion of the democratic potential of professional work in the age of measurement.

## Disclosure statement

No potential conflict of interest was reported by the author.

## Acknowledgement

An earlier version of this article was presented as invited keynote lecture at the Annual Conference of the Philosophy of Education Society of Australasia, Melbourne, 6–9 December 2013. I would like to thank the programme committee for the invitation. I would like to thank participants at the conference and the anonymous reviewers for helpful feedback.

## References

Aristotle. (1980). *The Nicomachean ethics*. Oxford: Oxford University Press.

Ball, S. (2003). The teacher's soul and the terrors of performativity. *Journal of Education Policy, 18*, 215–228.

Biesta, G. J. J. (2004). Education, accountability, and the ethical demand: Can the democratic potential of accountability be regained? *Educational Theory, 54*, 233–250.

Biesta, G. J. J. (2007). Why "what works" won't work: Evidence-based practice and the democratic deficit in educational research. *Educational Theory, 57*(1), 1–22.

Biesta, G. J. J. (2009a). Good education in an age of measurement: On the need to reconnect with the question of purpose in education. *Educational Assessment, Evaluation and Accountability, 21*, 33–46.

Biesta, G. J. J. (2009b). What is at stake in a pedagogy of interruption? In T. E. Lewis, J. G. A. Grinberg, & M. Laverty (Eds.), *Philosophy of education: Modern and contemporary ideas at play* (pp. 785–807). Dubuque, IA: Kendall/Hunt.

Biesta, G. J. J. (2010a). *Good education in an age of measurement: Ethics, politics, democracy*. Boulder, CO: Paradigm.

Biesta, G. J. J. (2010b). Why 'what works' still won't work: From evidence-based education to value-based education. *Studies in Philosophy and Education, 29*, 491–503.

Biesta, G. J. J. (2012). Giving teaching back to education. *Phenomenology and Practice, 6*, 35–49.

Biesta, G. J. J. (2013). Learning in public places: Civic learning for the 21st century. In G. J. J. Biesta, M. de Bie, & D. Wildemeersch (Eds.), *Civic learning, democratic citizenship and the public sphere* (pp. 1–11). Dordrecht: Springer Science+Business Media.

Biesta, G. J. J. (2014). *The beautiful risk of education*. Boulder, CO: Paradigm.

Bingham, C. (2008). *Authority is relational*. Albany, NY: SUNY Press.

Björkman, J. W. (1982). Professionalism in the welfare state: Sociological saviour or political pariah? *European Journal of Political Research, 10*, 407–428.

Carr, D. (2000). *Professionalism and ethics in teaching*. London: Routledge.

Charlton, B. G. (2002). Audit, accountability, quality and all that: The growth of managerial technologies in UK universities. In S. Prickett & P. Erskine-Hill (Eds.), *Education! Education! Education!—Managerial ethics and the law of unintended consequences* (pp. 13–28). Exeter: Imprint Academic.

Faulks, K. (1998). *Citizenship in modern Britain*. Edinburgh: Edinburgh University Press.

Feinberg, W. (2001). Choice, autonomy, need-definition and educational reform. *Studies in Philosophy and Education, 20*, 402–409.

Freidson, E. (1994). *Professionalism reborn: Theory, prophecy, and policy*. Chicago, IL: University of Chicago Press.

Hellín, T. (2002). The physician–patient relationship: Recent developments and changes. *Haemophilia, 8*, 450–454. doi:10.1046/j.1365-2516.2002.00636.x

Kunneman, H. (1996). Normatieve professionaliteit: een appèl [Normative professionality: An appeal]. *Sociale Interventie, 3*, 107–112.

Laing, R. D. (1960). *The divided self: An existential study in sanity and madness*. Harmondsworth: Penguin.

Laing, R. D., & Esterson, A. (1964). *Sanity, madness and the family*. London: Penguin Books.

Latour, B. (1987). *Science in action: How to follow scientists and engineers through society*. Milton Keynes: Open University Press.

Leaton Gray, S. (2007). Teacher as technician: Semi-professionalism after the 1988 Education Reform Act and its effect on conceptions of pupil identity. *Policy Futures in Education, 5*, 194–203.

Lyotard, J.-F. (1984). *The postmodern condition. A report on knowledge*. Manchester: Manchester University Press.

Meirieu, P. (2008). *Pédagogie: le devoir de résister* [Education: The duty to resist] (2e édition). Issy-les-Moulineaux: ESF.

Mouffe, C. (2000). *The democratic paradox*. London: Verso.

O'Neill, O. (2002). *BBC Reith lectures 2002. A question of trust.* Retrieved from http://www.bbc.co.uk/radio4/reith2002

Sarfatti Larson, M. (1979). *The rise of professionalism: A sociological analysis.* Berkeley, CA: University of California Press.

Slavin, R. (2002). Evidence-based education policies: Transforming educational practice and research. *Educational Researcher, 31,* 15–21.

von Braunmühl, E. (1975). *Antipädagogik* [Anti-education]. Weinheim: Juventa.

# Valuing and Desiring Purposes of Education to Transcend Miseducative Measurement Practices

R. Scott Webster

**Abstract**

*The separating and isolating tendencies of measuring practices can lead educators to lose sight of the aims and purposes of education. These end purposes can be used to guide and ensure that the activities of educators are educational, and therefore, Biesta recommends there is a need for educators to reconnect with them. This article. explores this notion of a 'reconnection' and argues that if educators are to challenge any potentially miseducative measuring practices, then this reconnection must require educators to value and desire particular end purposes. Desires are recognised to be existential in character and are identified as being necessary for initiating actions. It is argued here that this aspect of desires is important for understanding the significance of a 'reconnection' because without it the purposes of education may remain only as abstract philosophical ideals. To make a difference and to challenge the isolating and miseducative tendencies of some measuring practices, educators must come to value particular purposes of education, and in addition, they must exercise the courage to enact them. This can be made possible because educators strongly care for and desire the actualisation of the purposes to which they are connected.*

**Introduction**

Biesta (2010) describes our time as an 'age of measurement' due to the hegemonic practices of obtaining measured evidence mainly for the express purpose of improving 'performativity' (Lyotard, 1984). This affects schools and universities, and impacts teaching and research. In a recent discussion about teacher quality, the chair of the Australian Institute for Teaching and School Leadership Limited (AITSL), Tony Mackay (2014), expressed that such a discussion must be accompanied by asking 'how do we measure …teacher quality?' [my emphasis]. Similarly, Roberts and Peters (2008, p. 86) observe that 'the only research that counts' in neoliberal times 'is measurable research' [original emphasis]. It is argued here that the measuring practices which are dominating our age aggressively marginalise concerns of a more significant nature, such as considering the end purposes of (quality) teaching, schooling and education. The consequence of this dominance is that educators may be losing sight of education and its ultimate end purposes, and yet these are needed to guide and ensure activities are educationally valuable.

Measuring practices are recognised by Dewey (1988a, p. 33) to require specification, and he identifies that this may lead to particular elements like learning outcomes becoming 'isolated' from their relations to other elements such as aims and purpose of education. While this might make measuring practices easier, such a separation contributes towards a means–ends dichotomy where the technical means of measurement become separated from the overall end purposes which give measuring activities their value. This is potentially problematic because elements, such as learning outcomes, may be pursued because they are measureable and not because they are educative. Indeed it is becoming difficult for educators to distinguish between educative and miseducative activities because the current hegemonic measuring culture discourages engaging with the end purposes of education which can provide the criteria to make such a distinction.

Dewey (2008a, p. 11) reminds us that not all learning is educative. Some learning, like indoctrination, is miseducative where attitudes such as boredom, callousness and closed-mindedness emerge and which narrow opportunities for further growth. Determining whether learning is educative or miseducative requires an engagement in normative validity. This involves critically validating practices in terms of how they contribute towards particular purposes considered to be valuable as well as the evaluation of intended and unintended consequences as per consequential validity. These sorts of validation clearly involve engaging with the aims and end purposes of education. Only through an evaluation that is inclusive of end purposes, is the value of the consequences of particular learning activities and measured evidence able to be judged as educative or not. Normative validity is rarely promoted or practiced in educational institutions and so it is argued by Biesta (2010) that educators ought to reconnect with end purposes of education. This article shall explore further this notion of a reconnection by examining some existential aspects related to the very being and identity of educators.

## The Role of Individual Educators

Understanding measurements requires interpretation, which does not only identify factual information but it simultaneously involves making evaluative judgements. This is recognised by Putnam (2002) who demonstrates that all scientific inquiries depend upon the value judgements of the scientists themselves. Feyerabend (1993) even describes the methods of science as being driven by the Kierkegaardian 'passion' of the scientists. The judgements of scientists and of educators who seek to obtain measurements are based upon them personally accepting that the purposes of measurement are 'good' and valuable, and therefore worth their efforts. For example, obtaining measurements as evidence of particular learning outcomes for determining whether a certain teaching strategy is effective—and therefore possibly of 'quality'—assumes that the phenomenon of 'quality teaching' is real and can be measured and also that it is a valuable phenomenon worthy of being measured.

Educators are being encouraged to accept that there is value in the things they have been told to measure, rather than them valuing *educational* concerns which may or may not lend themselves to measurement—such as thinking and being moral. Giving up on, or ignoring educational ideals so as to comply with the requirements of this age of measurement, could be considered as living by Sartre's 'bad faith' because their identity as educators is compromised by complying with the demands of neoliberal managerialism. This is recognised by Biesta (2010, p. 12), who asks, are we 'valuing what we measure or measuring what we value?' This diversion of attention onto the how of attaining evidence via measurement has replaced concerns relating to end purposes of *education*. These end purposes provide the criteria *why* we ought to value certain things and Biesta recommends that we must reconnect with these. Bauman and Donskis (2013, p. 140) also recognise this lack of connection and refer to the 'corporate professor' who is 'strangely inarticulate about the purposes and worth of higher education'. In the light of this, Giroux (2014, p. 17) adds that 'academics have become overly comfortable with the corporatization of the university' and have become an active part of this ever-growing hegemonic culture of measurement leading to the loss of education and of democracy.

Eric Fromm (1981, p. 13) makes the interesting observation that knowledge of great ideas are now more widespread than they ever have been, but unfortunately 'never were these ideas less effective than they are today'. He argues that great ideas need to be lived if they are to have any impact on the world. Therefore, it is argued here that an important aspect of this reconnection to which Biesta refers, must include the elements of desire and commitment in order that they may become actualised. Interests and desires are considered to be central to an educator's identity. While it is recognised by Bauman (2004, pp. 37, 76–77) that identity is 'a hopelessly ambiguous idea' and 'a hotly contested concept' that unfortunately has served to replace 'the war for social justice' with 'a plethora of battles for recognition', identity is nevertheless considered here to offer a useful point of focus for pursing the enacting of educative practices. This is possible via an existential understanding of identity where one's activities are guided by meaningful and valuable end purposes which one has critically chosen and is passionate about. Identity in this sense can be understood through Giddens (1991, p. 35) as knowing 'both what one is doing and why one is doing it'. According to Taylor (1989, p. 27), our identity includes where we stand, our commitments and the 'framework' which provides the horizon from which we determine 'what is good, or valuable' and 'what ought to be done'. This understanding can be understood as existential, authentic and pragmatic where an emphasis is given to the primacy of individuals participating in the achievement of their identity as a mode-of-being rather than as an essence that can be objectified. This means that as individuals, we ought to connect with purposes of education in such a way that they become 'mine'.

For educators, this existential understanding of ourselves is significant because as Dewey (1985, p. 114) recognised, there are no grand universal aims of education to which we must comply but rather aims of education which are to be lived are only to be found with each individual person. This is reflective of Kierkegaard's (1992) notion of subjective truth which he used to represent the inwardness of each unique person to live one's own ideals as passionately as one can with a purity of will. Consequently, because aims and purposes of education function as ideals to which we as individuals aspire and care about, Dewey argued that these ought to be intelligently critiqued and considered. This involves more than just cognition for a reconnection. It also involves our whole being, especially our desires and how we value. This is why Dewey advices us to have our desires 'cultivated' so that as educators we come to desire significant end purposes for education.

**Current Culture of Measurement: Separating Means from Ends**

In this age of measurement, performativity has become the hegemonic discourse marginalising all other aspects which relate to education—particularly moral philosophy, political theory (Giroux, 2014) and of concern for us—*educational* research (Roberts & Peters, 2008). These latter aspects are intimately involved in end purposes, particularly the *ultimate* purposes which give all educational activities their direction and value. In this article , the contention with this 'age of measurement' is not measurement itself but rather it is the separation of measurement practices from the end purposes for which they are employed. Measurements can certainly be very valuable as they have added rigour and precision to countless inquiries which have in turn enriched our lives in various ways. The processes of measurement have also proven invaluable to research—including educational research. However, in this age of measurement, educators are being encouraged to give attention only to the means of measuring to the point where these have been isolated from bigger picture purposes of education and democracy. Consequently, this has resulted in a separation—where there is a foregrounding of the *means* of measuring and a relegation into the background of the *ends* or purposes of education.

The attempted separation of means from ends is particularly associated with a myopic focus upon effectiveness and performativity. This view is supported by Blake, Smeyers, Smith, and Standish (2000, pp. 90–91) who argue that '[p]erformativity eclipses deliberation about ends' and the excessive managerial focus on technical efficiencies and effectiveness causes 'discussion of ends and values …to be …relegated to the margins of education'. This marginalisation of aims and purposes of education has been recognised by several educational theorists. Noddings (2003) for example refers to discussions about end purposes as 'aims-talk', and she claims that in recent years, this has almost disappeared even from educational theory. Taubman (2009) and Biesta (2006) identify that accompanying this demise of engaging with educational aims and end purposes is an increased focus upon *learning* (in particular learning outcomes or objectives) instead of *education*. Consequently, it is the learning 'sciences' which are often called upon to provide the carefully measured evidence upon which best practices can be copied and applied.

The learning sciences are mostly to be found in the field of educational psychology. According to Taubman (2009, p. 195):

> The learning sciences offer the possibility that there exists, just beyond reach, that one final way of ensuring learning, for as Bransford, Darling-Hammond, and LePage write, "There are systematic and principled aspects of effective teaching, and there is a base of verifiable evidence or knowledge that supports that work. In that sense it is like engineering or medicine." (2005, p. 12)

This quote from Bransford et al. which Taubman cites appears neutral at one level in trying to uncover 'effective' principles of learning generally, but it nevertheless undervalues the nature of the context as one which specifically deals with human persons and not inanimate objects. Consequently, it is considered here to share some similarities with the behaviourist Edward Thorndike (1910, p. 6). In the first edition of The Journal of Educational Psychology, Thorndike wrote,

> A complete science of psychology would tell every fact about every one's intellect and character and behaviour, …It would aid us to use human beings for the world's welfare with the same surety of the result that we now have when we use falling bodies or chemical elements. …we shall become masters of our own souls as we now are masters of heat and light. (Thorndike, 1910, p. 6)

Here, we witness the high hopes of those in the learning sciences who seek the evidence of principles and procedures which can *cause* people to learn. Not only is the aspiration to ensure learning occurs, but such learning is also to be effective and efficient. However, Taubman (2009, p. 195) asks '[w]hat if the obsession with learning keeps us on track but also keeps us from being educated?'

An example of this means–end dichotomy is found in the school effectiveness movement. Pring (2004, p. 13) argues that the literature and research into the effective school 'ignores the question "Effective for what?"'. There is often an inferred 'good' in the notion of effectiveness so sometimes there appears to be an assumption that the more there is the better things will be. Such a view is reflected in Australia's Victorian Department of Education and Early Childhood Development's (2008, 2013) literature which promotes effective schools, effective teachers, effective learning, effective curriculum, effective leadership and effective feedback, but at no time does it offer an explanation as to why such effectiveness might be good and for what purposes. 'Effectiveness' by and of itself is self-referencing—things are effective when they are *effective*—which tells us very little other than there is an economic interest of profitability present involving the ratio of inputs to outputs. Lyotard (1984) and Apple (2004) describe this pursuit of efficiency as one which focuses on optimal performance by maximising outputs such as learning outcomes and minimising inputs such as paying teachers, without concern for what might be true, just or beautiful. However, it is these latter concerns which are pertinent to *education*. Lyotard (1984, p. 46) concludes that for educational practices, 'the goal is no longer truth, but performativity—that is, the best possible input/output equation'. He identifies that this notion of performativity is essentially positivistic because it assumes a closed and stable system with static parameters so that the input/output ratio can be carefully measured.

## How Educational Work is Being Affected

An important consequence of the attempted separation between means and ends is that measurement practices come to be understood within closed-systems ways of thinking and operating. This results in producing a narrow range of parameters which restrict what features educators can give to their consideration. This closed-systems approach typically confines issues of validity only to epistemological and technological concerns, and ignores (or actively avoids) the broader and deeper normative dimension which engages educators with consequences in relation to ultimate end purposes for practices including measuring activities. For example, the Whitlam Institute's report, *The Experience of Education: the impacts of high stakes testing on school students and their families* examines Australia's National Assessment Programme—Literacy and Numeracy (NAPLAN) in which the authors conclude that 'NAPLAN is not in the best interests of young Australians' (Wyn, Turnbull, & Grimshaw, 2014, p. 3). Here, the evaluation is made with reference to the overall 'good' for the students across the country. In contrast, the government department responsible for NAPLAN—the Australian Curriculum, Assessment and Reporting Authority (ACARA, 2014)—responded to this report by stating that they disagree with the findings in this report claiming it to be 'unhelpful' because their main concern is only to welcome 'feedback which is directed at improving NAPLAN'. Clearly from the response of this government department, we witness a focus upon the means of measurement—i.e. the NAPLAN test instrument itself, but this is accompanied by a complete neglect of engaging with broader concerns such as the value of the consequences that this testing activity might be having upon students' well-being.

When authorities tend to focus exclusively upon measurements such as national testing, they encourage a means–ends dichotomy. They do this by cajoling educators to focus upon the means as if these were good-in-themselves without having the need to reference end purposes beyond the measuring activities. This attempt to ascribe value to an activity or entity without referencing the consequences or relations to end purposes is an attempt to ascribe value in an absolute sense, as if the essential nature of a measuring instrument or activity has value in itself irrespective of its consequential impacts. In addition to NAPLAN testing, we can recognise other entities in educational literature which are imputed to have value in themselves such as intelligence, multiple intelligences, learning, technology and even knowledge. Consequently, these are presented as if they are isolated and self-evident 'goods' which do not require connection or justification to end purposes beyond themselves to give them their value.

This closed-systems approach clearly has an impact on how knowledge itself is understood. In the study conducted by Belenky, Clinchy, Goldberger, and Tarule (1997) on the intellectual development of women as knowers and how they view themselves and the potential of their own voices, these researchers found that those women who function at the most basic level (termed basic dualism) see their identity as being passive recipients of authoritative knowledge. These women understand knowledge as absolute and quantitative in nature rather than as something qualitative—there are no shades of grey but only blacks and whites. Statements of knowledge are considered factually true and 'trying to know "why" is not thought to be either particularly possible or important' (ibid., pp. 28, 41). Their research reflects the findings of William Perry's (1999, p. 71) study in which he too discovered that those who hold to 'discrete right-wrongs... [and] good-bads' restrict persons to understanding knowledge in terms of quantity, preventing them from considering 'a genuinely qualitative meaning of "better and worst"'. Believing knowledge to consist of discrete and objective facts leads to a passive relation between the knower and the known. In order to transcend this and to become a more responsive and responsible thinker, the subjects in his studies developed an appreciation that knowledge is relational and as knowers, they individually accept responsibility to give sense, legitimacy and value to what they know.

The most basic level of intellectual development of dualistic thinking identified by Perry (1999) and by Belenky et al. (1997) involves placing certainty in knowledge. This same tendency has also been identified by Dewey (1929) as being significantly problematic for creating an assumed divide between persons as (subjective) knowers and (objective) knowledge. This contributes to a spectator theory of knowledge, and according to Dewey, this appears to have accelerated since 'the Cartesian definition of quantity as the essence of matter' came to dominate Western thinking such that 'the resolution of objects in nature as a whole into facts stated exclusively in terms of quantities... [has signified] that this is the effective way to *think* things...' (ibid., pp. 92, 134). This separation between knowers and knowledge has contributed to the most basic stage of knowing as identified by both Perry (1999) and Belenky et al. (1997), where 'thinking' is reduced to passively mimicking what is assumed to be the essence of knowledge which primarily has a quantifiable nature able to be separated from values and purposes.

This spectator theory of knowledge as exemplified through the basic dualistic mode of thinking has led to another attempted separation which significantly affects the identity of educators. This other assumed separation is between thinking and doing. According to Brown, Lauder, and Ashton (2011), in corporate institutions where effectiveness and performativity are highly valued, educational workers are considered to be 'doers' but not 'thinkers' in the sense that the knowledge which they disseminate to student–clients does not require any qualitative intervention via their expert input, interpretation or evaluation. Digital Taylorism is able to calculate performance and efficiencies of educational workers through the measurement of pre-determined learning outcomes. This is made possible due to the imputed quantitative character of knowledge enabling it to be reduced to 'components, modules and competencies' (ibid., p. 77).

This reduction of knowledge into quantitative components and the redefining of education as an activity involving the 'delivery' of curriculum by teachers and the accumulation of learning outcomes by students is described by Barnett (1994, p. 71) as 'an epistemological assault on the very character of what counts as reason in the university'. He identified four ontological deficiencies which are produced as a result of reducing knowing and understanding of students to observable outcomes and competencies. These include:

1. As educators, we do not know the intentions, interests and desires of students by looking solely at their observable behaviours;

2. Our view of what it means to be human is challenged by assumptions which separate thought and action;
3. The concept of 'work' which involves the personal meaningfulness and authenticity of workers, is replaced by 'labour' which only consists in externalised competencies and performances; and
4. Through the loss of acknowledging the relation between action and thought, there is a total neglect of the appreciation that all actions are 'saturated with thought'. (Barnett, 1994, pp. 76–77)

These deficiencies tend to fragment the identity of educators from being intimately connected with the lives of their students, from giving thought to actions and from critically engaging with the purposes of education which give meaning and direction to all of their activities.

Barnett (1994, p. 77) argues that these four ontological deficiencies have produced 'an impoverished view of human action' which ought to be remedied by an approach which appreciates that *education* consists of 'a combined intellectual and ethical affair'. This is in line with the scheme developed by Perry titled 'Forms of ethical *and* intellectual development' to acknowledge the qualitative nature of the relation between knowing and valuing. Perry (1999, pp. 170–181) argues that the most advanced positions in his scheme are characterised by persons who understand that the activity of knowing is more 'qualitative rather than structural' and as such involves personal responsibility in taking a stance and for being personally committed to some overall purpose. Perry argues that what is required to operate at this highest position in his ethical and intellectual scheme is courage, especially moral courage, to take responsible action amongst the complexities of various and sometimes conflicting value systems. This is considered significant for the identity of educators if we are to transcend the potentially miseducative practices in this age of measurement.

## The Importance of Dewey's Ends-In-View

Dewey (2008b, p. 235) reminds us that '[n]o human activity operates in a vacuum'. This is because we are purposeful beings who engage in activities which have some *value* because of their consequences and how these relate to other interests. Otherwise, we might consider that we 'appraise' an activity (a means) because it is considered to have absolute value in itself. The act of honesty might be considered as a prime example of an assumed value in itself, and it can even be labelled as a virtue in order to emphasise its importance. Similarly, a purpose (an end) can be considered to be 'prized' because it is believed to have value in itself such as '*effective learning*'. However, it is argued here that both means and end purposes have value primarily because of their relation with each other and that these relations, relating together in a holistic network, are a significant part of our identity. Dewey (2008b, p. 218) explains that 'there is union of prizing and appraising' through what he terms as an *end-in-view*. He explains that an end operates like a target or a goal to be aimed at but simultaneously and importantly it also provides direction for the sort of means that are appropriate for *hitting* the target (Dewey, 1985, p. 112). As an object the target actually provides direction and guidance by giving purpose to the activity of hitting the target. These targets or goals can also be used to determine the value of particular activities which lend themselves as means for reaching the target and therefore to judge whether they are appropriate for such a task.

Both the end purposes and the means of attaining these purposes are considered valuable because of their *relation* with each other. But this relation does not exist as a closed system but necessarily must also involve other significant interests and purposes which are affected through the consequences of the activities. So the virtue of honesty, for example, might be given value because of the consequences it produces both in terms of the results of the activity upon elements beyond the person being honest and also for the internal consequences regarding what sort of person one becomes by exercising this virtue. However, if there was a situation where being honest would mean revealing to a brutal murderer the location of a potential victim, then the consequence might determine that honesty may not have value if justice, protection of the vulnerable and the constraining of evil are also desired as valuable ends or 'targets'. Desiring particular end purposes signifies personal involvement and commitment and these are necessary actions that are to be initiated. Therefore, the role of desire is considered here to have great importance for educators if they are to actively resist hegemonic measurement practices which marginalise education.

Through Dewey's notion of an end-in-view, we can understand how his theory of valuation presents 'value' as a verb rather than as a noun because similarly to hitting a target, valuing is the direction that is given to pursue the means for attaining worthwhile end purposes. Consequently, he argues that objects, such as diamonds, are given value because of the human activities in which they are involved (Dewey, 2008b, p. 194). Similarly, we understand that objects such as Australia's NAPLAN test are given value through the activity that they are assumed to be supporting as a means for attaining some worthwhile end purposes. However, the *relations* between particular measuring activities, as *means*, and the ends which give them value, are often actively ignored.

Indeed if the personnel in managerial roles were to articulate the end purposes which guide many of their measuring activities, they would predictably identify in many instances that they are expressly to satisfy their interests for accountability in terms of performativity and efficiencies (Blake et al., 2000; Ravitch, 2010; Roberts & Peters, 2008; Taubman, 2009). Such reasons which provide the justification for the many measuring practices in education are clearly embedded within the discourse of business management and as such, this may work against the discourse of education (Webster, 2012). Some concerns for efficiencies are certainly legitimate and do have a role to play in the life in all organisations. However, Dewey argues that what is important to recognise is that thoughtful deliberation over competing values, and attempting to determine which might be more valuable than others in particular situations, is a necessary characteristic of evaluation—or normative validity—and tends to be absent from 'the business mind' which Dewey (1988b, p. 29) describes as 'not itself unified' because it is disconnected from concerns relating to social development and the public good. This latter aspect clearly involves qualitative concerns regarding which overall purposes and consequences are better and why they might be better and is not of a quantitative sort as warned by Perry (1999) and Belenky et al. (1997) which reduces such considerations to being simple matters of either right or wrong, good or bad.

Normative validity requires thinking of a qualitative kind which reaches to and critically engages with ultimate purposes. As the activity of thinking relates to the relevance, an activity has in relation to a particular purpose, prolonged thinking engages with many such relations of relevance. Dewey's (2008b) theory of valuation is theory of relevance in this sense and, as such, is central for being an educated person. Evaluating and thinking through a network of total relevance requires educators, as inquirers, to have a way-of-being that is both authentic and democratic. Dewey argued that this ontological aspect of our identity is more important than the actual 'things' that we assume to 'know'.

A significant aim of education pertains to the sorts of people students are becoming. This ontological focus involving the identity and *being* of persons (rather than on quantifiable knowledge and skills which might be obtained and acquired like commodities) is considered by Eric Fromm to involve a different mode of understanding personhood and education. Fromm (1976) argues that *being* and *having* are two different modes of existence which directly influence our way-of-being. He draws on Kierkegaard's notion to 'will one thing' to argue for the importance of committing oneself 'to a goal' (Fromm, 1992, p. 31) to explain the importance of having one's whole life being directed and guided by significant purposes which give value to one's activities. This clearly better enables educators to resist falling victim to bad faith by participating in measuring activities might be miseducative. Fromm (1976, p. 111) also describes this as a 'religious attitude' by arguing that 'we are what we are devoted to, and what we are devoted to is what motivates our conduct'. The thing which gives our life significance is what Fromm (Fromm, 1947, pp. 15, 17) describes as a 'vision of the end' which is not so much to be obtained or arrived at, but rather offers guidance on how we 'ought to live' and is therefore an intrinsic aspect of our identity and who we are. As such this is very much like Dewey's end-in-view which offers direction to our activities like a target offers direction to the activity of hitting it. The following section shall take up this theme of devotion by examining the notion of desires and the importance of having these educated or 'cultivated' in order that our lives might be guided by significant purposes and not just any purposes, appetites or impulses. This is considered especially important for the identity of educators because, drawing on Dewey, Garrison (Garrison, 2010, p. xiii) argues 'We become what we love. Our destiny is in our desires'.

**Educating Our Desires**

If educators are to challenge and change the problematic aspects of the current hegemonic measurement culture of our age such as the separation of knowers from knowledge, doing from thinking, facts from valuing, teachers from students, the intellectual from the ethical and means from ends, then they ought to 'reconnect with the question and purpose of education' as Biesta (2010, p. 26) recommends. This reconnection is essential if we are to transcend the isolating and miseducative tendencies associated with measuring practices. It is argued here that in order for such a 'reconnection' to occur and for it to make a difference, educators must come to *desire* particular end purposes for education. Purposes help give value to activities and it is contended here that they must be *desired* if educators are to become committed and able to exercise the courage to initiate important actions even if they are perceived by some authorities as being disobedient (Fromm, 1981) rather than passively complying to managerial requests to simply measure. Commitment to end purposes or ends-in-view consisting of aspirations and philosophical visions enables educators be to be more efficacious and resilient (Australian Council of Deans of Education, 2014). It may therefore assist some educators from becoming victims of neoliberal managerialism which, as Giroux (2014) has observed, is consuming many, if not most academics.

The importance of personal desires and interests are found throughout the works of Dewey (2008b, p. 204) where he clearly identified that 'valuation involves desiring'. That is, in order to value and to evaluate, end purposes must be referenced as criteria and must also be desired as worthwhile. The intellectual factor involved in critical and thoughtful inquiry needs a certain energy to enable a person to become committed and moved to take action. This is recognised by Ronald Barnett (2007, p. 59) who represents this through the concept of the 'will' and argues that the will works alongside reason to 'energise' it. He explains that the will is central to our identity and being. It can be described as a 'spirit' due to its aspirational and teleological character and because it propels us forward helping to provide commitment, energy and purpose to invest ourselves into certain activities. It is recognised through the capacity of persons to apply effort and discipline in order to pursue the goals that they consider to be worthwhile. This notion of the will or spirit is, according to the existentialist Kierkegaard (1989), central to the identity of persons because it holistically gathers all that we are connected with into a meaningful way of life or way-of-being that gives sense to all of our activities. This is why Barnett (2007, p. 15) argues that the 'will' 'is the most important concept in education' because it is necessary in the ongoing transformation of free and critical persons.

Dewey explained that 'desires' are quite different to 'wishes' because of the energy and effort involved in striving after their actualisation, whereas wishes can be made quite wistfully and even in despair as Kierkegaard argued. This makes Dewey's understanding of 'desire' similar to Barnett's conceptualisation of the will which he too characterised as involving effort and discipline. Dewey warned against passively implementing practices dictated to us from authorities who impose their own purposes on us without the inclusion of our thinking about and desiring them because this is akin to becoming like a 'slave' (Dewey, 1985, p. 90). In addition to this challenge from external authorities, Dewey also warned us not to passively comply with the already existing desires within ourselves that have not firstly been carefully examined and critiqued. He was against people seeking to satisfy their own 'natural' desires, appetites and impulses because the consequences that result from having these satisfied often inevitably produce consequences which are not in our long-term best interests or the best interests of others. Kierkegaard (1992) was also aware of the need to critically and seriously 'choose ourselves' by uncovering and challenging our internal purposes and desires. Dewey (1988c, pp. 132–133) encourages us to challenge and 'cultivate' our interests and desires in order to develop worthy or 'desirable' ends-in-view and explained that,

> The 'desirable', or the object which *should* be desired (valued), does not descend out of the a priori blue nor descend as an imperative from a moral Mount Sinai. It presents itself because past experience has shown that hasty action upon uncriticised desire leads to defeat and possibly to catastrophe. The 'desirable' as distinct from the 'desired' does not then designate something at large or a priori. (Dewey, 2008b, p. 219)

We can appreciate the importance of Dewey's (2008b, p. 221) 'intellectual factor' which is present in the activity of an inquiry. End purposes ought to have critical thought invested into them so that educators can first understand the reasoning as to why particular purposes might be better than others. Then educators can commit themselves to these purposes and strongly desire them because they have been convicted on an intellectual level. But this critically thoughtful endeavour to establish worthwhile purposes requires energy and effort as recognised by Barnett and Dewey who acknowledge that it is easier to simply wish or to accept purposes given to us from others. Dewey argued that,

> The chief difficulty with adults is very much like that from which children suffer in schools. We do not know what we really want and we make no great effort to find out. We, too, allow our purposes and desires to be foisted upon us from without. (Dewey, 1988c, p. 133)

Here, Dewey challenges us not to succumb to the easier option of simply adopting activities which have been separated from their primary purposes and which others assume we ought to adopt. Activities, including measuring activities, which are worthy of our desires and commitments are those which have had our own personal, free and serious thought invested into their end purposes and consequences. This assists us to develop ultimate concerns regarding how we understand what might be educative and worthwhile. Dewey understood that end purposes have an existential nature due to the personal commitment which is involved and are significantly important for making good judgements and decisions, for living relatively good lives. He explained that this was the case with Plato and argued that '[u]nless we know the end, the good, we shall have no criterion for rationally deciding what the possibilities are which should be promoted' (Dewey, 1985, p. 94). Such criteria are necessary for conducting normative evaluations regarding ones activities in education.

Importantly, Dewey recognised that the desires that we have towards some particular purposes are often fuelled when we need to address some problem. He claimed that 'desires arise only when "there is something the matter," when there is some "trouble" in an existing situation' (Dewey, 2008b, p. 220). He therefore values interruptions to habitual ways of conduct because these interruptions may initiate an inquiry to address and re-evaluate the 'trouble'. This is captured in Biesta's (2006, p. 150, 2010, p. 90) notion of a 'pedagogy of interruption' in which the subjectivity of persons, the very uniqueness of each individual, is called to give 'a responsive and responsible response' to a provocation usually in the form of a question which asks and challenges 'what do you think about this?' and 'where do you stand on this?' Such interruptions offer a 'call' to respond to a previously unacknowledged or unappreciated situation. The importance of such responses for educators is to assist them in being clear regarding what they do and why they do certain things. Biesta argues that as a pedagogy, this interruption opens up people to be better able to engage with living and with existence. Hence, he argues that its strength is primarily existential.

It is argued here that this existential dimension is crucially important because it signifies the potential value for what it might mean for becoming educated in such a way that lives become more meaningful. The pedagogy of interruption brings to the conscience of each person how s/he relates to and makes sense of all that s/he does and this can be provoked by an emerging 'trouble'. Existentially this is significant as Kierkegaard (1983, pp. 274–275) argues that consciousness only becomes present when there is contradiction or conflict. These contradictions and conflicts are often between one's ideals and understandings on the one hand, and one's actual reality and activities on the other hand. An example of this being evoked would be to interrupt and challenge ourselves as educators to reflect upon our activities for measurement and assessment, and to examine what the consequences and purposes of such activities might involve and whether we would evaluate them to be worthwhile in terms of our ideals for education. The discriminating and critical judgement that must be exercised to resolve this 'trouble' would uncover where we stand intellectually regarding what is most important for us in our *educational* practice. Uncovering our desires which energise us to take action would reveal how we are oriented existentially to give value to all of our activities.

Perry's scheme of intellectual and ethical development draws upon the work of Dewey who argued throughout his works about the importance of a certain kind of educated, critical and democratic mode of individuality which was needed to oppose the rampant, self-interested individualism of his day. He labelled this individualism as Americanisation and characterised it as consisting of quantification, mechanisation and standardisation. He considered that the America of his time was living in a corporate age where individuals were encouraged to conform to 'the crowd' causing authentic individuality to become lost where people 'cannot be captains of their own souls- their beliefs and aims' (Dewey, 1988b, pp. 67, 82–83). He argued that these lost individuals 'will refind themselves' when their ideals engage more rigorously with the realities of their enacted lives. This is the same argument advanced by Kierkegaard to seek conflict and new insights through engaging our ideals with our present activities as mentioned in the above paragraph.

The existential and educative interest of Kierkegaard and Dewey is to break out of habitual modes of recollecting and having our lives dominated by inherited meanings from the past, and to seek possibilities and to test for their potential value. For both Kierkegaard and Dewey, the *interest* and *desire* of the individual are paramount. Interest and desire are often understood as 'care' or as 'will' by Barnett. This existential dimension is significantly important because it operates in-between ideal end purposes and actual 'real' activities and therefore positions the individual in relation to how s/he stands in relation to these two aspects in such a way that s/he comes to value and desire particular and purposeful ways-of-being (Caputo, 1987, pp. 33, 300).

## Conclusion

It has been argued here that educators must be 'connected' and if necessary—'reconnected' to all of their activities (especially when measuring and assessing) in such a way that they are conscious of how their actions might be understood to have value in terms of end purposes for education to which they desire and are committed. By being existentially connected to ultimate aims and purposes of education educators will strive to avoid miseducative practices and ensure that they assess what they value rather than be seduced into valuing only what is required by authorities to be measured. Therefore, reconnecting with significant end purposes of education is considered an educative process in itself as well as being necessary for educators to assist them educating others.

In this age of measurement, elements such as learning outcomes and test scores are separated and isolated in order to be measured. This has led many academics and teachers to lose connections between assessment activities and purposes of *education* which are necessary if activities are to be considered as valuable in terms of education. This requires that educators learn to critically inquire into what purposes of education might be most worthwhile and also to *care* about such ends. Giving sense and value to our practices and activities in education requires us to be connected to and interested in end purposes.

The recent trend in this age of measurement which promotes separation has witnessed the loss of such connection, interest and care. It has been argued here that if educators are to actively challenge miseducative practices which are characteristic of an excessive measuring culture, then they must come to have their desires for particular end purposes of education 'cultivated' and strengthened. This requires consideration to be given to potential conflicts between what is desired to occur and what are actually the activities which are being required by neoliberal managers. For example, we ought to be 'troubled', to use Dewey's term, that over deterministic approaches to measuring which often reduce students to a numerical grade or essentialised 'style' of being a learner, loses what it means to be a human person in a unique, rich and valuable way.

Dewey recognised that courage is required for the process of critical valuation because it involves all of one's being. He argued that 'democracy involves individual responsibility for judgement and choice' and that this 'is a strenuous doctrine that demands courage of thought and belief for realisation' (Dewey, 1988c, p. 135). Indeed he considers that 'the primary requisite of critical ability is courage' (ibid., p. 134). This is because the embodiment of intellectually knowing and valuing particular end purposes of education may inevitably lead to actions and activities which are directed to attaining these ends and yet which may differ, challenge and confront the accepted and expected practices of a culture. However, if the hegemonic practices of the age of measurement which are focussed exclusively on performativity are to be challenged and changed, then an education of the desires, will and courage of educators is needed.

## Disclosure statement

No potential conflict of interest was reported by the authors.

# References

Apple, M. W. (2004). *Ideology and curriculum*. New York, NY: Routledge Falmer.
Australian Curriculum, Assessment and Reporting Authority. (2014). *ACARA rejects conclusions of the Whitlam Report*. (Released 19th May 2014 at http://www.acara.edu.au/20140519_the_whitlam_report.html)
Australian Council of Deans of Education. (2014, June). *Teaching for excellence: ACDE submission to the teacher education ministerial advisory group*. Retrieved from http://www.acde.edu.au/publications/
Barnett, R. (1994). *The limits of competence*. Buckingham: The Society for Research into Higher Education and Open University Press.
Barnett, R. (2007). *A will to learn*. Buckingham: The Society for Research into Higher Education and Open University Press.
Bauman, Z. (2004). *Identity*. Cambridge: Polity Press.
Bauman, Z., & Donskis, L. (2013). *Moral blindness*. Cambridge: Polity Press.
Belenky, M. F., Clinchy, B. M., Goldberger, N. R., & Tarule, J. M. (1997). *Women's ways of knowing*. New York, NY: Basic Books.
Biesta, G. J. J. (2006). *Beyond learning*. Boulder, CO: Paradigm Publishers.
Biesta, G. J. J. (2010). *Good education in an age of measurement*. Boulder, CO: Paradigm Publishers.
Blake, N., Smeyers, P., Smith, R., & Standish, P. (2000). *Education in an age of nihilism*. London: Routledge Falmer.
Brown, P., Lauder, H., & Ashton, D. (2011). *The global auction*. Oxford: Oxford University Press.
Caputo, J. D. (1987). *Radical hermeneutics*. Bloomington Indianapolis: Indiana University Press.
Department of Education and Early Childhood Development. (2008). *Blueprint for education and early childhood development*. Melbourne: Author.
Department of Education and Early Childhood Development. (2013). *From new directions to action*. Melbourne: Author.
Dewey, J. (1929). *The quest for certainty*. New York, NY: Minton Balch & Company.
Dewey, J. (1985). Democracy and education. In J. Boydston (Ed.), *John Dewey: The middle works*, 1899–1924 (Vol. 9). Carbondale: Southern Illinois University Press.
Dewey, J. (1988a). The sources of a science of education. In J. Boydston (Ed.), *John Dewey: The later works*, 1925–1953 (Vol. 5). Carbondale: Southern Illinois University Press.
Dewey, J. (1988b). Individualism, old and new. In J. Boydston (Ed.), *John Dewey: The later works*, 1925–1953 (Vol. 5). Carbondale: Southern Illinois University Press.
Dewey, J. (1988c). Construction and criticism. In J. Boydston (Ed.), *John Dewey: The later works*, 1925–1953 (Vol. 5). Carbondale: Southern Illinois University Press.
Dewey, J. (2008a). Experience and education. In J. Boydston (Ed.), *John Dewey: The later works*, 1925–1953 (Vol. 13). Carbondale: Southern Illinois University Press.
Dewey, J. (2008b). Theory of valuation. In J. Boydston (Ed.), *John Dewey: The later works*, 1925–1953 (Vol. 13). Carbondale: Southern Illinois University Press.
Feyerabend, P. (1993). *Against method*. London: Verso.

Fromm, E. (1947). *Man for himself*. Greenwich, CT: Fawcett Publications, Inc.
Fromm, E. (1976). *To have or to be?* London: Continuum.
Fromm, E. (1981). *On disobedience*. New York, NY: HarperCollins.
Fromm, E. (1992). *The art of being*. New York, NY: Continuum.
Garrison, J. (2010). *Dewey and eros*. Charlotte, NC: Information Age Publishing, Inc.
Giddens, A. (1991). *Modernity and self-identity*. Stanford, CA: Stanford University Press.
Giroux, H. (2014). *Neoliberalism's war on higher education*. Chicago, IL: Haymarket Books.
Kierkegaard, S. (1983). *Fear and trembling and repetition*. (H. V. Hong & E. H. Hong, Trans.). Princeton, NJ: Princeton University Press.
Kierkegaard, S. (1989). *The sickness unto death*. (A. Hannay, Trans.). London: Penguin.
Kierkegaard, S. (1992). *Concluding unscientific postscript to philosophical fragments*. (H. V. Hong & E. H. Hong, Trans.). Princeton, NJ: Princeton University Press.
Lyotard, J.-F. (1984). *The postmodern condition: A report on knowledge*. Minneapolis: University of Minnesota Press.
Mackay, A. (2014). *Enhancing teacher quality through professional standards*. The Australian Institute for Teaching and School Leadership Limited (AITSL). Retrieved May 30, 2014 from http://www.ceo.aitsl.edu.au/blog/enhancing-teacher-quality-through-professional-standards#comments
Noddings, N. (2003). *Happiness and education*. Cambridge: Cambridge University Press.
Perry, W. G. (1999). *Forms of ethical and intellectual development in the college years: A scheme*. San Francisco, CA: Jossey-Bass Publishers.
Pring, R. (2004). *Philosophy of education*. London: Continuum.
Putnam, H. (2002). *The collapse of the fact/value dichotomy and other essays*. Cambridge, MA: Harvard University Press.
Ravitch, D. (2010). *The death and life of the great American school system*. New York, NY: Basic Books.
Roberts, P., & Peters, M. A. (2008). *Neoliberalism, higher education and research*. Rotterdam: Sense Publishers.
Taubman, P. M. (2009). *Teaching by numbers*. New York, NY: Routledge.
Taylor, C. (1989). *Sources of the self*. Cambridge, MA: Harvard University Press.
Thorndike, E. L. (1910). The contribution of psychology to education. *Journal of Educational Psychology, 1*, 5–12.
Webster, R. S. (2012). Challenging student satisfaction through the education of desires. *Australian Journal of Teacher Education, 9*, 80–92.
Wyn, J., Turnbull, M., & Grimshaw, L. (2014). *The experience of education: The impacts of high stakes testing on school students and their families*. Penrith: The Whitlam Institute within the University of Western Sydney.

# Getting the Measure of Measurement: Global educational opportunity

PENNY ENSLIN AND MARY TJIATTAS

**Abstract**

*Although measurement is widely misused in education, it is indispensable in addressing the problems of injustice in global educational opportunity. Considering how the case can be made for legitimate use of measurement in normative analysis and argument, we explore ways in which metrics have featured in the formulation of theories of justice, with particular attention to resourcist and capabilities approaches. We then consider three means of addressing global inequality and defend a reconstruction of the public sphere in which objective measures of justice, deliberatively constructed, could supersede prevalent assumptions about measurement.*

## 1. The Use and Misuse of Measurement

> Not everything that counts can be counted and not everything that can be counted counts. (Einstein, attributed by Scott & Light, 2004, p. 135)

Too many issues, activities, procedures and standards in education are corrupted by the inappropriate use of numerical measurement. The spectacular achievements of mathematics and physics in creating order through accurate measurement of time, distance, weight, height, length and speed have, unsurprisingly, encouraged social scientists, psychologists and educators to emulate such success. Pursuit of mechanical measures of quality is pervasive, and has infiltrated educational institutions (as manifested for example in the prominence of citation indices in the evaluation of academic research and league tables in rating schools and universities). The appeal is not difficult to explain. Given the importance of education as a factor affecting individual life-choices, an objective, scientific measure of quality is considered to be invaluable. 'The seductiveness of such measures is that they all turn measures of quality into measures of quantity, thereby allowing comparison across cases with a single metric' (Scott & Light, 2004, p. 119).

The *seeming* availability of a univocal, objective measure is, according to Scott and Light, one important aspect of the problem: the measures are of questionable validity since they do not capture what they purportedly are concerned to measure—viz., quality. But the deeper concern, they note, is that democratic forms of reasoning about standards and the value of knowledge fall prey to technical calculation lacking in scientific validity and moral justification (p. 119). Even if the scientific validity of the measures could be secured (presumably by employing sound rules of aggregation and selecting correct metrics that would provide relevant information), this would not be a sufficient guarantee of reliability. This is because such measures 'colonize' behavior (Scott & Light, 2004, p. xx), creating new kinds of ways for people to be. Such concerns do not show that numerical information has no role in a process of reasonable deliberation. But Pogge sums up the obvious caution well: we should be aware of 'carefully made-up statistics that keep us comfortably ignorant of what we are doing' (Pogge, 2010a, p. 2). We need to employ established and proposed measures cautiously, and remain vigilant with respect to their role in public deliberation.

Despite these cautions, we argue that some things that count can and should be counted. By various measures, global poverty and associated inequality in educational opportunity are an injustice. In Australia, the country ranked second on the Human Development Index (HDI) in 2012, life expectancy at birth was 82 years, while mean years of schooling enjoyed by Australians was 12 years. By contrast, in bottom-of-the-table Mozambique, life expectancy was measured at 50.7 years and mean years of schooling 1.2 years (United Nations Development Programme [UNDP], 2013). Similar raw disparities are evident in the huge differences in educational expenditure and participation rates between developed and developing countries reported in the monitoring reports of the Education for All campaign, in association with the Millennium Development Goals (e.g. UNESCO, 2013/2014).

Even more compelling evidence of the power of measurement of inequality, because it brings out the way in which numbers can indicate significance and potential for action, is the evidence that Pogge (2010a) presents about global poverty and what quite modest redistribution from developed to developing countries could do to relieve it:

> Although 48 percent of the world's population, 3085 million human beings, were reportedly living below [the World Bank's $2.50 a day] poverty line in 2005 ... their collective shortfall from this line amounts to only 2 percent of global household income. A 2 percent shift in the distribution of global household income could wholly eradicate the severe poverty that currently blights the lives of nearly half the human population. (Pogge, 2010a, p. 12)

Numerical measurements like these say a lot about global inequality, in which poverty and education are closely interrelated. The high levels of literacy and numeracy that are essential to development 'come only with free and compulsory public education' (Okin, 2003, p. 290). In many situations education can contribute to increased incomes. When children's labor is necessary to household income they are likely to go without education. If malnourished or ill and unable to afford treatment they may miss school or learn less successfully. 'If a woman works a seventeen hour day, she cannot take advantage of the literacy program that might otherwise improve her earning power or enable her to find out about her legal rights or government programs or services she could qualify for' (Okin, 2003, p. 305).

Inequalities in educational opportunities between rich and poor countries, we have argued (Enslin & Tjiattas, 2004), imply cosmopolitan duties of justice that require global redistribution of educational resources. In focusing now on the role of measurement in pursuit of more just global educational opportunities, we explore the significance of quantitative information when asking distributional questions. Numbers are clearly important in handling such questions, for justice is largely about distribution (Enslin & Tjiattas, 2009). So numerical information is apt, if not indispensable. And numerical indices allow for it to be presented in a form that is amenable to policy and decision-making in large-scale contexts.

Yet in view of widespread recognition that numerical measures have been misused in the service of promoting questionable objectives in education, how can a case be made for their legitimate use in normative, and especially moral, analysis? Our discussion begins (sect. 2) with an illustration of the way in which metrics have featured in the formulation of theories of justice in political philosophy. Specifically, we examine the ways in which Rawls and Sen conceptualize the metric of social justice, survey more applied accounts of their theories, and proceed to analyses of what Pogge calls 'morally plausible' indices of equity. Arguing for a widened notion of *counting*, we then explore (sect. 3) three means of addressing global inequality. We defend a reconstruction of the public sphere in which objective measures of justice, deliberatively constructed, could supersede prevalent assumptions about measurement (sect. 4). In defending measurement, understood both qualitatively and quantitatively, normatively and numerically, as having an important role in deliberations about justice in education, we suggest that debates about the appropriate metric of justice are, crucially, about the normative foundations of justice.

## 2. Justice: Which Metric?

### 2.1. Some Preliminaries

The justifiability of distributional principles depends in part on the rules of aggregation they employ, as brought out in discussions (e.g. Parfit, 2013; Scanlon, 1998) about the justifiability or otherwise of additive aggregative principles of reasoning, most prominently employed in utilitarian thought, which attempts to measure the goodness of states of affairs by summing benefits and harms across individual lives and discounting distributional considerations. Utilitarianism often functions as the paradigmatic way of giving numerical considerations significance in practical reasoning. But its prominence is also responsible for the prevalent assumption that allowing numbers to count in normative deliberation is *inevitably* accompanied by a non-distributional view of the goodness of states of affairs. However, as several philosophers insist, these should be taken to be independent considerations.[1]

The important point here is that indices, used 'as proxies for values that political actors of various kinds purport to measure' (Pogge, 2010a, pp. 76–77), required in order to evaluate and compare states of affairs, need to be constructed so that they reflect, isolate and point to, and amalgamate morally relevant factors. As such, indices are inescapably normative. In political philosophy, indices are readily associated with the work of such prominent figures as Rawls, Sen and Pogge. In Rawls's succinct formulation (1982, p. 364), the index of primary goods 'defines a public basis of interpersonal comparisons for questions of social justice'. Of course, as he himself points out (1982, p. 373), evaluations making use of indices are variable. '... we make interpersonal comparisons in many different contexts and for many different purposes; each context has its relevant considerations according to the appropriate ends in view. On birthdays we give things that we know are wanted, or that will please, to express affection ...' Citizens (conceived as free and equal moral persons) require primary goods, and justice requires distribution according to those needs (Rawls, 1982, p. 374). Since we are centrally concerned with principles of distribution, we are concerned with those theories which primarily evaluate states of affairs with respect to just distribution.

Our central question is thus, 'What is the proper metric of justice?' In other words, 'What should we look at when evaluating whether one state of affairs is more or less just than another?' (Brighouse & Robeyns, 2010, p. 1).

*2.2. Resources or Capabilities*

Theories of justice, which have set out to provide independent, cross-cultural measures of the goods required for well-being, are an obvious source of candidates for the proper metric of justice. The most well-known and influential of all, Rawls's (1971) account of just distribution, explicitly includes an index of primary goods (basic liberties, powers and prerogatives of offices of responsibility, income and wealth and social basis of self-respect), or resources, those goods which anyone would need, whatever else they wanted, the all-purpose means to a wide variety of ends, and the principles according to which these are to be distributed. Such an index, Rawls believes, allows us to make interpersonal comparisons with respect to social justice (1982, p. 359). Rawls's hypothetical contractors in the original position, behind a thick veil of ignorance, are given the task of choosing, in the form of principles of justice, fair terms of cooperation. The index of primary social goods serves, for them, as a 'thin theory of the good', which they use to measure their life-long prospects, how well off they would be, regardless of who they turn out to be when the veil is lifted. The use of primary goods in making interpersonal comparisons in questions of social justice rests on the conception of moral persons (Rawls, 1982). Parties '... best represent citizens as free and equal moral persons by deciding between alternative principles of justice according to how securely these principles provide for all citizens the primary goods' (Rawls, 1982, p. 366). Justice requires distribution according to citizens' needs *as free and equal moral persons* who try to realize their conceptions of the good. The principles of justice are rules that determine how these goods are to be distributed.

Anderson (2010) helpfully breaks down the two main constituents of theories of distributive justice: they must, she insists, specify two things: *a metric*, which characterizes the type of good subject to demands of justice, and *a rule* that determines how the good should be distributed. Different theories of justice may thus be compared with respect to these: utilitarianism proposes a subjective metric (happiness and preference satisfaction) as opposed to both Rawlsians and capability theorists who propose objective metrics (resources and functionings, respectively). Deliberations about social justice can never dispense with qualitative reasoning; counting can never be a proxy for this, although it can be a very useful aid to reflective evaluation (Anderson, 2010). Questions about the metric of social justice attempt to find out what the appropriate informational basis of evaluations should be taken to be. Sen (2009, p. 291) reminds us that 'Every normative theory of social justice demands equality of something—liberty, income, equal treatment of everyone's rights'. It proposes an informational focus or metric: utilitarianism concentrates on individual happiness, pleasure, or 'utility' as the best way of assessing individual well-being, Sen (2009) takes capability as a basic informational ingredient, and Rawls believes social primary goods provide the informational basis for evaluations concerning just distribution. Ultimately, the plausibility of the metric is intrinsically tied to the theory of justice from which it derives. Theories of justice also provide rules about how the goods specified by the metric are to be distributed to meet requirements of justice. Rawlsians and capability theorists propose procedural and distribution-sensitive rules, while utilitarians insist on rules that sum and maximize the good—and are pattern-insensitive.

Rawls's theory provides for assessment of outcomes that is much more complex than the simple additive aggregation of utilitarianism. Fairness is a function not simply of the maximization of happiness or desire satisfaction, but, crucially, of their distribution, and goods are defined with respect to what citizens require in order to realize their nature as moral persons.

The now standard alternative to Rawls's metric is provided by the 'capabilities approach' of Sen and Nussbaum, who propose that the 'currency of justice' is fundamental human capabilities or functionings, rather than social primary goods. The latter, they believe, in failing to track the diverse ways in which people are able to use goods to achieve their ends, stops short of ensuring well-being and the opportunity to realize positive freedom (Nussbaum, 2007; Sen, 2009). This is because people have varying needs for resources and different abilities to convert resources into functioning. The value of resources lies in how they promote human functioning: the focus in evaluating just distribution is on the personal characteristics (capabilities or substantive freedoms) that govern conversion of primary goods into a person's ability to promote her ends, rather than on a standard set of resources at her disposal. Sen has argued that the primary goods metric is too inflexible to take account of the diversity of needs, varying with health, longevity, and location. Thus, for Sen, the Rawlsian metric, which focuses on means rather than on actual opportunities of living, fails to capture the differential advantages enjoyed by people with different capacities to convert primary goods into functionings, and so allows for 'unjustified inequality' (Sen, 1990, p. 112). For both Nussbaum and Sen the 'space' of justice is that of capabilities, rather than opportunities.

We shall not attempt to adjudicate the dispute about the reducibility or otherwise of one of these positions to the other, but we do take them to be notational variants, differing in emphasis or on minor details.[2] Both are illuminating when applied to justice in education. Education viewed in Rawlsian terms as a social primary good is also likely to lead to the acquisition of other primary goods like employment and income. A resourcist approach is amenable to measurement of opportunity, in the form of expenditure, school attendance, provision of classrooms, learning materials and qualified teachers. The capability approach in turn exposes some limitations of a resourcist view of educational opportunity by showing how persons are differently placed to benefit from educational opportunities, by varying personal attributes and circumstances that may favor or impair their converting opportunities into outcomes. The capability approach demonstrates that outcomes in the form of capabilities and functionings, which are less amenable to numerical measurement, are also a crucial facet of equal opportunity. But learning outcomes can be especially vulnerable to educationally inappropriate forms of measurement that colonize and corrupt what they are supposed to promote. And some intrinsically valuable benefits of educational opportunities, whether formal, non-formal or informal, are not measurable by any index.

*2.3. Objectivity and Metrics*

Sen asks: 'In what way can diagnosis of injustice or identification of what would reduce or eliminate it be objective?' Demands of objectivity call for objective reasoning in thinking about issues of justice and injustice (Sen, 2009, p. 41), and in turn to public reasoning (2009, p. 122). Sen recognizes the importance of Rawls's work (e.g. 1971) in drawing attention to the point that judgements of justice cannot be an entirely private affair, and that a 'public framework of thought' is critically important. Both Rawlsian and capability theories of justice are committed to objective notions of the good in matters of just distribution. This is a major difference between them and utilitarian accounts of justice. They both hold that the standard of objectivity of ethical principles is 'basically congruent with their defensibility within a public framework of thought' (Sen, 2009, p. 134). But several commentators (e.g. Pogge, 2010b) have pointed out that Sen's insistence on a public framework is in tension with the insistence on sensitivity to the variable capacity sought by capability theorists. Pogge (2010b) believes that capability theory does not yield an informationally workable metric, because it cannot function as a public criterion of social justice. Kelly (2010) concurs that Sen's proposed metric does not seem to lend itself to the construction of a public common standard of measurement for interpersonal comparisons as readily as Rawls's (1971) notion of primary goods: Rawls thus provides a much stronger basis for meeting the publicity requirement. Kelly finds it difficult to conceive of '… how a common standard of measurement could be constructed' if claims of distributive justice focused on welfare or 'functionings' (2010, p. 62). On the other hand, the notion of primary goods '… provides a public and readily quantifiable measure for interpersonal comparisons'. In addition, by circumventing appeals to contested conceptions of the good, the metric of primary goods provides a basis for public decision-making.

*2.4. Morally Plausible Metrics*

There is a growing interest among political and policy theorists in indices, both as instruments for aggregating information and as standards of evaluation. But if indices are to capture phenomena of normative interest (e.g. poverty, gender equality) rules of aggregation and metrics need to be appropriate so as to base evaluations on relevant information.[3]

Sen's landmark work, *Development as Freedom* (1999) is an incisive critique of many World Bank policies and led to changes in how the UN measures development (in various *Human Development Reports* from 1990 onwards). For Sen, meaningful development cannot be equated with economic growth '... or measured in the readily calculable ways preferred by most economists, but must take account of how people are capable of functioning ...' (Okin, 2003, p. 289). Development is gauged instead with respect to the expansion of people's freedoms.

Due to the work of Sen and his colleagues, the capability approach has been operationalized by UN and various national governments and adopted by many policymakers and economists. The capability approach has enjoyed much attention and influence, having captured the attention of international agencies and nongovernmental organizations, largely as a result of the fact that the United Nations Development Program (UNDP) has adopted scores on the HDI, which is a capability metric worked out in collaboration with Sen, rather than GNP per capita as its official comparative measure.

More generally, development economists are now rethinking goals and measurement of economic development. Okin points to work that registers the neglect of '... well-being, freedom, capacities, functioning and voices of the world's women, especially the poorest' (Okin, 2003, p. 288). The 'feminization of global poverty', Okin claims, has not been well served by standard economic measures that take the family as their basic economic unit and do not disaggregate data with respect to individual members. Treating each household as a 'black box', these measures have failed to detect the extent of gender inequality, since they are insensitive to intrafamily distributions. In addition, economic productivity is measured in terms of labor, goods, services bought and sold in the marketplace, and excludes measurement of reproductive labor.

The HDI allows for quality of life comparisons across nations to be made in a way that captures data about individual rather than aggregate well-being. Annual *Human Development Reports* use concepts of functionings and capabilities as one of their theoretical cornerstones (UNDP). More than 500 regional *Human Development Reports* have been published. In Britain work done for the Equality and Human Rights Commission builds on and extends the capability approach (e.g. Equality & Human Rights Commission, 2011).

Some critics like Pogge (2010a), however, believe that the UN's HDI, though apparently more comprehensive and multidimensional (degree of development of each nation is calculated as the average of three components: life expectancy at birth (L), education (E), and gross domestic product (GNP) per capita (P)), is still defective insofar as it is a measure that applies to countries rather than individuals. It fails to capture information about distribution within populations. It does not capture the extent and depth of human deprivation. Of most concern is that flawed indices misdirect policy makers (Pogge, 2010a). Pogge's positive suggestion is that, in order to do better in constructing indices, interpersonal aggregation should be performed only after the relevant aspects of each person's situation have been holistically assessed. The idea is that a holistic measure of individual deprivation, grounded in a sound conception of basic human needs/requirements/capabilities, can be used in a range of different aggregation exercises without swamping information concerning individuals and their circumstances.

Recent *Human Development Reports* have responded to criticisms of early constructions of the HDI, changing the factors taken into account, the weighting of factors, and how they relate to one another. The HDI also acknowledges the need for measurement of poverty within developed states: the 2013 *Human Development Report* observes (p. 2), that '[t]here is a south in the north and a north in the south'.

## 3. Making What Counts Count

### 3.1. What Counts, Who Counts?

Despite Einstein's warning (Scott & Light, 2004, p. 135) against the assumption that all things that count can be counted and conversely that all things that can be counted count, the evidence of recent debates about metrics of justice suggests to us that some important things that count can be counted and that if informed by proper philosophical reflection the counting is getting better. Perhaps 'we are at least working in the right place and looking at the right thing', as Nussbaum observes of the *Human Development Reports* (Nussbaum, 2002, p. 135). As indices improve and debates about their merits embrace wider publics, so we could reduce the chances of colonizing the very goods and outcomes that we set out to measure, in addressing both global poverty and the unequal educational opportunity that it reflects and reproduces.

The Education for All *Global Monitoring Reports* present evidence of both the dangers of colonization and of refinement of indices used to measure inequality and progress in alleviating it. Although the number of children not in school fell by almost half from 107 million to 57 million between 1999 and 2011 (UNESCO, 2013/2014), states' pursuit of enrolment targets has been at the expense of quality education, for the basics have not been learned by an estimated 250 million children (UNESCO, 2013/2014). Looking ahead to the post-2015 framework, the 2013/2014 *Global Monitoring Report* implicitly responds to the colonization effect generated by targeting bigger numbers of children in schools, observing that the emphasis has as a result shifted from increasing enrolments to regarding quality education as central. While enrolments have improved, pupil–teacher ratios have barely changed. Raw enrolment measures will need to be read alongside progression rates, data on completion of primary school, and assessments of learning. Children in countries that do not yet produce these kinds of measures are not counted, nor are children not in school in countries that do produce data on assessments of learning taking place in schools. Much more work needs to be done to disaggregate the data, e.g. to 'distinguish clearly between children from advantaged and disadvantaged households' (UNESCO, 2013/2014, p. 91).

Whatever progress has been achieved so far, the Millennium Development Goal of universal primary education as 'Education for All' will not be achieved. As noted earlier, in comparing measures of poverty and access to schooling in Australia and Mozambique, vastly unequal resources and opportunities indicate that global redistribution is needed. Redistribution of resources would create enhanced opportunities to develop literacy, numeracy, information, skills and the critical perspectives individuals and societies need to exercise their will through their participation in global public reason, as well as in viable economies, on equal terms with others. Such public reason, if it includes debates about global justice, its metrics and measures, will require a numerate and literate global population.

Further progress towards better measures, in the sense of both indices and associated policies, demands a widened notion of counting. As well as being critically vigilant about counting what can both be counted and is worth counting, who counts, how do they count, and under what conditions is the counting done? We bear these underlying questions in mind in now discussing what measures ought to be taken to create a global order that measures up normatively, considering three means of addressing inequalities in the global distribution of resources: redistribution through individual and institutional action; structural changes in the global order; and counting the voices of the poor.

*3.2. Redistribution*

Global inequality is huge and growing, both between countries (Pogge, 2010a) and between rich and poor within countries (Piketty, 2014). Possible remedies to global inequalities between countries have been proposed by both resourcists and capability theorists, as well as by utilitarians (e.g. Singer, 2009). One such remedy is explicitly distributive, for example Pogge's (2010a) claim that the poverty gap could be erased if global household income were redistributed by a shift of 2%. Varying measures have been proposed to effect such a shift. Recommending that rich nations agree to allocate 1% of their GDP to address this gap, Nussbaum (2004, p. 16) argues that *Prosperous nations have responsibility to give a substantial portion of their GDP to poorer nations* (emphasis in original), as they have responsibilities to develop the capabilities of citizens of poorer countries as well as their own. Young (2011) supported the view that absolute poverty in the world could be eliminated if only the richest nations were to devote 0.7% of GNP to and for the world's poor.

Redistribution of wealth from rich to poor countries could take the form of voluntary contributions by individuals (Singer, 2009). Voluntary philanthropy on the part of those who can afford to give does pose some practical problems, such as which charitable organizations can be trusted to direct donations to those most in need and for projects that do improve the conditions of the world's poorest people. A well-rehearsed philosophical problem is how we might ensure that all who could contribute will do so; why would some who can afford to contribute do so if others similarly placed decline to do so? Global poverty is a structural problem that demands structural solutions, not one that can be adequately addressed through individual action.

*3.3. Structural Change*

In his account of the kinds of institutional reforms that would count, Pogge is skeptical about the role of individual action through such measures as affluent citizens' donations. Because the international rules that govern national and international economic transactions 'are the most important causal determinants of the extent and depth of severe poverty and other human rights deficits' (2010a, p. 52), global structural reform rather than 'aid' is his preferred option. It would also cost affluent citizens less and would be more likely to be supported than donations. This kind of agency requires at least that global citizens in rich countries exercise institutional negative duties, because 'citizens may be implicated when social institutions they uphold foreseeably produce an unavoidable human rights deficit on a regular basis' (2010a, p. 29). Such deficits, Pogge argues, can be attributed to institutional factors. These include both the actions of global institutions and institutional arrangements in developing countries, controlled by economic and political elites for their own gain, frequently with the connivance of multinational companies, and agencies and governments of developed countries, e.g. through bribery and resource privilege (2010a, pp. 47,48). Structural reforms, 'Even small changes in the rules governing transnational trade, lending, investment, resource use, or intellectual property can have a huge impact on the global incidence of life-threatening poverty' (p. 53; see also p. 55).

Nussbaum (2004) believes that we all share a collective duty to address the entitlement of all human beings to the development of the capabilities[4] she lists. But she too regards creating appropriate institutional structures as more suitable than looking to individual efforts (2004, pp. 14–15)—including among these structures domestic organizations, multinational corporations, agencies like the World Bank and International Monetary Fund, the UN, the World Court, as well as NGOs, in a *thin, decentralized, yet forceful global public sphere* (2004, p. 16, emphasis in original). Such a global public sphere should enable the voices of the poor to be heard and to count.

*3.4. Taking the Voices of the Poor into Account*

The global poor count not only as deserving of remedial action by rich countries' individual citizens, as well as by governments and NGOs, and also corporations and global bodies that have tended to serve the interests of the developed north. A strong case has been made by both philosophers and the authors of the *Human Development Reports* that the voices of the poor must count in public debate about remedial change to address their needs.

Okin's account of evidence about 'what the people who comprise the least well-off quintile think about their own most pressing needs' (2003, p. 280) supports the view that listening to their voices is indispensable to addressing global injustice. Policy and practice in economic development have excluded the perspectives of the poor, especially those of women. The 1990 *Human Development Report* identified the need to hear women's voices early in the development of the Human Development Index, remarking (UNDP, 1990, p. 32): 'Women count—but are not counted'. Okin insists too that GDP does not measure development and that measured growth does not measure poverty reduction. Significantly for our purposes, she notes how frequently studies that do listen to the voices of the poor, especially those of women, report their wish for educational opportunities, for themselves and for their children. Nussbaum (2002, p. 135) presses support for listening to the voices of the poor further, in the direction of democratizing measurement itself: 'We need to rely on the ingenuity of those who suffer from deprivation: they will help us find ways to describe, and even to quantify, their predicament'.

Voice continues to feature strongly in recent *Human Development Reports*. The 2013 Report emphasizes the importance of enabling citizens, including the youth, to participate by giving voice to their views and needs (UNDP, 2013). Unjust governance systems compound unjust and inequitable socio-economic conditions because they are monopolized by the wealthy and the powerful, excluding the voiceless (p. 37). The *Human Development Reports* often note the link between education and political empowerment: 'Trends conducive to empowerment include the vast increases in literacy and educational attainment in many parts of the world that have strengthened people's ability to make informed choices and hold governments accountable' (UNDP, 2010, p. 6).

## 4. For Good Measure: Disaggregating Global Political Structures

We have argued that measurement has a legitimate and necessary role to play in education, provided it is understood in normative as well as numerical terms. So, in considering measures of global inequality in the related spheres of poverty and education, indices are inescapably normative. Whether one employs a resourcist or a capabilities approach as a metric of social justice, both illuminate the task of devising objective means to measure justice and injustice, and offer a substantial improvement on the previously dominant utilitarian approaches. Furthermore, such objectivity demands a widened conception of counting as well as redistribution, structural change and a voice for the poor, as measures to address global inequality.

To complement our discussion, in sect. 2, of problems of aggregation in indices of poverty and inequality, we conclude by proposing a different form of disaggregation, of states as political units in which objectivity may be sought when public reason addresses inequalities and distribution of resources. For Pogge (2010a) the traditional distinction between international and intra-national relations is obsolete; hence he prefers the term 'global' to 'international' (p. 14). Charles Beitz's earlier groundbreaking extension of Rawls (1971) principles of justice to the global sphere points the way (Beitz, 1999, p. 199): choices, whether about institutions or policies, should consider impartially the claims of every person who could be affected.

Far from following this maxim, the world actually operates through institutions, from global to local, that 'apply to people largely without their consent and which have the capacity to influence fundamentally the course of their lives' (Beitz, 1999, p. 204). The integrated global economy makes it increasingly difficult to distinguish global institutional structures from domestic structures. This interdependence led

Beitz to influentially extend the theory of justice that Rawls intended for one society to a theory of global distributive justice, applying the difference principle both to the minimization of intrastate inequalities and 'to persons in the sense that it is the globally least advantaged representative person (or group of persons) whose position is to be maximized' (p. 152).

Switching the emphasis of justice, distribution, and so of politics itself from the entrenched idea of the world as comprising distinct societies constituted as states has radical implications not only for how people, poverty and unequal educational opportunities are counted. Nussbaum, Sen and Pogge, and Beitz (*inter alia*) envisage obligations of justice in a global politics extending beyond nation states. In this crucial respect they depart from Rawls (1971). They would all agree with Nussbaum's objection to Rawls that his statist position '… cannot defend redistribution from richer to poorer nations' (2004, p. 4). They would also insist that public reason is central to democracy and justice both domestically and *globally*.

Just as improved indices have required disaggregation of factors that previously seemed obviously aggregable, so too some disaggregation and reconstruction of organizations and publics responsible for counting will be needed. While much work remains to be done on feasible conceptions and structures for global democracy, several options have been put forward. Although there is widespread skepticism about the feasibility of creating formal global structures of governance (see e.g. Goodin, 2010), Held's (1995) theory of cosmopolitan democracy has, for example, proposed an elected assembly as an additional United Nations structure. Others (e.g. Bohman, 2007; Cohen & Sabel, 2004) have turned to the European Union as an emergent political order whose web of procedures, such as the Open Method of Coordination, enable citizens to debate EU policies across national boundaries with other EU citizens. Bohman has also explored the potential of public sphere theory for developing global democracy through forms of distributed communication across multiple *demoi* (Bohman, 2009). Much further disaggregation and reconstruction will need to take place, of publics and organizations that could enable the global order and particular democratic regimes measure up to the demands of justice. Whatever forms such spaces and structures ultimately take, achieving objective measures of justice, in education and elsewhere, is best understood as predominantly a normative, political matter, rather than a question of perfecting numerical indices.

## Disclosure statement

No potential conflict of interest was reported by the authors.

## Notes

1. In line with our own views in this article, Parfit (2013) for example has recently been at pains to show that by allowing numbers to count, we are not necessarily committed to discounting distributional considerations. The reason utilitarianism is deficient, he claims, is not because it gives weight to numbers, but because it ignores distributive considerations. A position which is duly sensitive to the latter, is not necessarily precluded from

taking numbers into account, or arriving at conclusions by aggregating different factors. Aggregation need not take the form of simple summing (see also Temkin, 2009, p. 3). The elements relative to goodness of lives or outcomes can be combined non-additively as well (as in principles that accommodate distributive considerations, like maximin, that privileges the welfare levels of the worst off, adopting the alternative whose worst outcome is superior to the worst outcome of any other alternative (Rawls, 1971)).

2. See Anderson (2010), where it becomes clear in her attempt to compare resourcist and capability views that they are aligned with respect to most of the central questions making up their respective theories. Pogge (2010b) more directly asserts that the list of key determinants of quality of life that Sen (1999) lists can be represented in resourcist theories—both, Pogge claims, share a commitment to normative individualism, to the individual as the ultimate reference point for evaluating institutional orders, and so to the same aggregative function, and are similarly opposed to sum-ranking aggregation of utilitarianism. More concretely, both capability and resourcist theories of justice disaggregate data, and so can evaluate intrafamily distributions. In addition, sophisticated resourcist theories are sensitive to diversity of social and environmental context.) Several commentators (e.g. Daniels, 2010) go further, arguing that the distinction between capabilities and opportunities is not clearly sustainable. The most significant difference that Daniels and Anderson independently identify is that capability theory insists on a more demanding opportunity principle, one which is sensitive to more aspects of disadvantage than Rawls's principle.

3. The World Bank provides, in Pogge's view clear examples of how not to use indices. For example, in recording information on household consumption it ignores household composition. He also objects to its practice of adjusting the international poverty line (IPL), by changing the base year for comparing the purchasing power of currencies, switching from talk of 'number' to 'proportion' in addressing the objective of halving poverty by 2015, because it patently misrepresents progress towards attaining the UN Millennium Development Goals (2010a, p. 58). Warning against apparent achievement of progress through statistical gimmicks, Pogge observes that:The steady stream of happy news that World Bank delivers from the poverty front—worked into the titles less anyone miss the point—is not robust with respect to the level at which the IPL is set. This discredits the method the Bank and the UN are using to track world poverty by counting the poor. (2010a, p. 65).

4. Nussbaum (e.g. 2007) lists ten capabilities: life; bodily health; bodily integrity; senses, imagination and thought; emotions; practical reason; affiliation; other species; play; control over one's environment.

## References

Anderson, E. (2010). Justifying the capabilities approach to justice. In H. Brighouse & I. Robeyns (Eds.), *Measuring Justice* (pp. 81–100). Cambridge: Cambridge University Press.
Beitz, C. (1997; 1999 edition with new afterword). *Political theory and international relations*. Princeton, NJ: Princeton University Press.
Bohman, J. (2007). *Democracy across borders: From demos to demoi*. Cambridge, MA: MIT Press.
Bohman, J. (2009). Democratization through transnational publics: Deliberation across borders. In R. Geenens & R. Tinnevelt (Eds.), *Does truth matter?* (pp. 149–165). Secaucus, NJ: Springer.
Brighouse, H., & Robeyns, I. (2010). Introduction: Social primary goods as metrics of justice. In H. Brighouse & I. Robeyns (Eds.), *Measuring justice* (pp. 1–13). Cambridge: Cambridge University Press.
Cohen, J., & Sabel, C. (2004). Sovereignty and solidarity: EU and US. In K.-H. Ladeur (Ed.), *Public governance in the age of globalization* (pp. 157–175). Farnham: Ashgate.
Daniels, N. (2010). Capabilities, opportunity, and health. In H. Brighouse & I. Robeyns (Eds.), *Measuring justice* (pp. 131–149). Cambridge: Cambridge University Press.
Enslin, P., & Tjiattas, M. (2004). Cosmopolitan justice: Education and global citizenship. *Theoria, 104*, 150–168.
Enslin, P., & Tjiattas, M. (2009). Philosophy of education and the gigantic affront of universalism. *Journal of Philosophy of Education, 43*(1), 1–17.
Equality and Human Rights Commission. (2011). *Developing the children's measurement framework: Selecting the indicators*. London: Author.
Goodin, R. (2010). Global democracy: In the beginning. *International Theory, 2*, 175–209.
Held, D. (1995). *Democracy and the global order*. Cambridge: Polity.
Kelly, E. (2010). Equal opportunity, unequal capability. In H. Brighouse & I. Robeyns (Eds.), *Measuring justice. Primary goods and capabilities* (pp. 61–80). Cambridge: Cambridge University Press.
Nussbaum, M. (2002). Capabilities and social justice. *International Studies Review, 4*, 123–135.
Nussbaum, M. (2004). Beyond the social contract: Capabilities and global justice. An Olaf Palme lecture, delivered in Oxford on 19 June 2003. *Oxford Development Studies, 32*, 3–18.
Nussbaum, M. (2007). *Frontiers of justice: Disability, nationality, species membership*. Cambridge, MA: Harvard University Press.
Okin, S. M. (2003). Poverty, well-being and gender. What counts, who's heard? *Philosophy & Public Affairs, 31*, 280–316.
Parfit, D. (2013). *On what matters* (Vol. 2). Oxford: Oxford University Press.
Piketty, T. (2014). *Capital in the twenty-first century*. Cambridge, MA: Harvard University Press.
Pogge, T. (2010a). *Politics as usual: What lies behind the pro-poor rhetoric?* Cambridge: Polity.
Pogge, T. (2010b). A critique of the capability approach. In H. Brighouse & I. Robeyns (Eds.), *Measuring justice* (pp. 17–60). Cambridge: Cambridge University Press.
Rawls, J. (1971). *A theory of justice*. Cambridge, MA: Harvard University Press.
Rawls, J. (1982/1999). Social unity and primary goods. In S. Freeman (Ed.), *John Rawls, collected papers* (pp. 359–387). Cambridge, MA: Harvard University Press.
Scanlon, T. M. (1998). *What we owe to each other*. Cambridge, MA: Harvard University Press.
Scott, J., & Light, M. (2004). The misuse of numbers. In J. Purdy (Ed.), *Democratic vistas* (pp. 115–137). New Haven, CT: Yale University Press.
Sen, A. (1990). Justice: Means versus freedoms. *Philosophy and Public Affairs, 19*, 111–121.
Sen, A. (1999). *Development as freedom*. Oxford: Oxford University Press.
Sen, A. (2009). *The idea of justice*. London: Allen Lane.
Singer, P. (2009). *The life you can save: Acting now to end world poverty*. New York, NY: Random House.

Temkin, L. (2009). Aggregation within lives. *Social Philosophy and Policy, 26*(1), 1–29.
UNESCO. (2013/2014). *Global monitoring report 2013/4: Teaching and learning: Achieving quality for all*. Paris: UNESCO.
United Nations Development Programme (UNDP). (1990). *Human development report 1990*. New York, NY: Oxford University Press.
United Nations Development Programme (UNDP). (2010). *Human development report 2010. The real wealth of nations: Pathways to human development*. Basingstoke: Palgrave Macmillan.
United Nations Development Programme (UNDP). (2013). *Human development report. The rise of the south: Human progress in a diverse world*. New York, NY: Author.
Young, I. M. (2011). *Responsibility for justice*. New York, NY: Oxford University Press.

# Creating the Civil Society East and West: Relationality, responsibility and the education of the humane person

JĀNIS (JOHN) TĀLIVALDIS OZOLIŅŠ

## Abstract

*A recurring theme in many places concerns the nurturing and maintenance of a civil society that is committed to justice, to human fulfilment and a community that actively pursues the good of all its members. The creation of a civil society where there is respect for persons and a concern for the good of others is an important social aim and though it is not the sole responsibility of educational institutions, they have a crucial role to play in its development. It also evident that the creation of a civil society includes the family and the wider community and so in order to understand how a civil society is to be fostered, we need to understand relationality, a central concept in both the Western and Eastern understandings of human nature. If we reflect on contemporary education in both the East and the West, an important question to consider is the extent to which education measures up to developing in young people a sense of their responsibilities to one another, their families and to the wider community. In short the question of how well we are developing humane persons who are able to relate to one another and build a civil society. This article argues that there needs to be a rebalancing of the aims of education to include the development of those values and dispositions that will foster a civil society.*

## Introduction

Although poverty, insecurity, instability and oppression are generally associated with developing nations and wealth, security, freedom and stability are associated with developed countries, if we look more closely at individual nations, we will see that poverty, insecurity, instability and oppression are not strangers in developed countries nor wealth, security, freedom and stability all missing from developing countries. The picture is much more complex than stereotypes suggest and there are inequalities in both. For a large portion of the world's population that lives in developing countries, the daily struggle to survive demands their utmost attention because grinding poverty saps away their optimism. There is no time to think beyond getting the next meal and hunger is too often fatal. Coupled with wars, famine and natural disasters, life are a daily struggle to survive. In wealthy countries, for one segment of the population, a surfeit of material possessions has led to new problems, such as obesity, heart disease, diabetes, a shallow self-absorption and a general dissatisfaction with life. Seduced by the neoliberal, capitalist promise that self-worth and fulfilment is to be found in the generation of profit and the accumulation of wealth for oneself to the exclusion of all else, many have been confronted with the meaningless of their lives. For others in the same wealthy countries, poverty, joblessness and insecurity are a fact of life and the gap between the rich and poor widens. In all parts of the world there is a thirst for justice, human dignity and respect, freedom and self-fulfilment. The so-called Arab Spring,[1] in which totalitarian regimes were swept away is a powerful symbol of the deep yearning that people have for a better life and a more just distribution of the common good.

Undoubtedly, for everyone the provision of the basic necessities of life through economic activity is a necessity, but it is evident that beyond a certain level, the possession of material goods becomes counterproductive in the search for human fulfilment and happiness. Aristotle's analysis in the *Nichomachean Ethics* of what is good for human beings remains as relevant today as it did over two thousand years ago. Aristotle recognised very clearly, firstly, that the good for human beings was to pursue happiness and this did not consist in fame, fortune or power, but in the acquisition of virtue (Aristotle, 1976). Secondly, in the *Politics*, he observed that human beings are social beings and that virtue is to be pursued within the family, the household and the State (Aristotle, 1981). In the East, Mengzi reaches the same conclusion. The good of human beings is to cultivate the virtues and this is to be understood in terms of the proper regard for others (Mencius, 1970). The virtues are to be pursued in the context of our relationships with others and it is through these that we are fulfilled as human beings and achieve happiness, which is our purpose in life.

Human beings, because they are social creatures, require the right kind of social structures to provide the habitat in which they can flourish and this is supplied by the community in which they live and work. In the sophisticated and complex world in which we live, the community has not only a private aspect, but also a public one. In the public sphere, human social organisation has three overlapping domains: the State, the market or economy and civil society. It is on the development of civil society on which we will focus, since it is this with which individuals have the most immediate relationship as it involves association with others. The creation of a civil society where there is respect for persons and a concern for the good of others, it is argued, is an important social aim and though it is not the sole responsibility of educational institutions, they have a crucial role to play in its development.

Given the dissatisfaction with life and cynicism that pervades attitudes to politics and the public sphere in general, there is an urgent need to examine how well our educational institutions are contributing to the development of civil society. It is critical, therefore, if we reflect on contemporary education in both the East and the West, to consider the extent to which education measures up in developing in young people a sense of their responsibilities to one another, their families and to the wider community. Arguably, the emphasis in contemporary education is on the gaining of skills to equip persons for a changing workplace and while this is not unimportant there are equally important values and dispositions that need to be cultivated. While some of these skills will include social skills, as social beings, being able to relate to one another and so to create a community which helps and sustains each of its members, is just as important as having useful skills. The centrality of this is recognised by philosophers in both the east and west, but these voices are not often heard. We will argue that there needs to be a rebalancing of the aims of education to include the development of those values and dispositions that will foster a civil society.

This rebalancing, however, is not easy, since we firstly need to have a clear conception of what we understand civil society to be, secondly an awareness of the importance of fostering our relationships with others in the formation of human and personal identity and thirdly, an appreciation of the difficulties in measuring our progress towards developing those values and dispositions that will lead to the achievement of civil society. We will begin with an account of civil society. It will be argued that, though the conception of civil society is fluid, it acts as an informal, complex but powerful counterweight to both the State and to the market.

Drawing on Chinese conceptions of civil society, we identify civic society as an aspect of civil society, arguing that it is the development of commitment to the values of civil society that serves both civic society and the transformation of communities. Because of his understanding of the power of education for the development of a transformative civil society, Gramsci's account of civil society is taken up. Its influence on individuals is direct, since it is made up of various associations, as Young indicates, including educational institutions, in which individuals interact and relate to one another. This leads us to reflect on the crucial nature of relationality in both Eastern and Western conceptions of human formation and to contend that being able to relate to one another is vital in the development of civil society and in turn in the development of personal identity.[2] Human beings come to understand their interconnectedness and interdependence through the institutions of civil society, especially educational institutions, and this, in turn, enables the fostering of a concern for social justice and the common good, both requirements for human flourishing. The impulse to transform society for the better occurs in both East and West, and one of the vehicles for this is civil society and its institutions. Though the interdependence of human beings seems obvious, it is at odds with the libertarian assertion of the paramount importance of individual autonomy and of laissez-faire economics. It is proposed that, while acquisition through education of skills and capacities is important, a rebalancing of the aims of education to include the cultivation of the virtues is necessary for a just and fair civil society in which all human beings can flourish. This demands reassessing the emphasis in educational curricula on skills and capacities that are measureable and a realisation that some of the most worthwhile values and dispositions that education cultivates are not amenable to measurement, but are nevertheless crucial for a civil society and for human well-being.

## What is Civil Society?

In recent times, attention has shifted from discussion of civil society to global civil society, but, like civil society itself, there is little consensus about what it means and it remains ill-defined (Evans, 2000; Kingsnorth, 2003; Milner, 2003; Taylor, 2004; Waterman, 1996). What it shares with civil society itself is the characteristic of there being organisations, such as International Non-government Organisations (INGOs), which operate outside the jurisdiction of States and directly with individuals, groups and associations within a country.[3] Defined as occupying a position somewhere between families, local communities, the State and the market, global civil society operates at a level that is transnational, transcending the boundaries of countries, their economies and local politics. Global civil society, however, does not consist only of INGOs and other global organisations, but also of a complex of sometimes loose global associations to which people belong and which are facilitated through social media. It is important to recognise the significance and growth of global civil society through the proliferation of various international associations, but if we are to understand global civil society we firstly need to understand civil society at the local level. It is generally held that civil society within a state will occupy a position between the State and the market. We will confine our discussion to civil society and its relationship to the State and market within a country.

In examining different conceptions of civil society, it is evident that these are many and varied, though not as ill-defined as global civil society. In Chinese, civil society is rendered 公民社会, (gongmín shè huì), people's society, and there are two other ways in which the term has been rendered, e.g. civil society in a legal sense is shì mín shè huì, 市民 社会 and mínjiān shè huì, 民间社会, which is civil society in the sense of Non-Government Organisations (NGOs) (Keping, Thornton, & Li, 2009, pp. 37–38). There is no consensus how these terms are to be used, though there is a distinction made between NGOs and other kinds of social organisations. Some NGOS will in fact have close contact with government and will have a quite overt political purpose. For example, these will include the China Women's Federation, the Chinese Communist Youth League and many trade unions (Keping et al., 2009, p. 40). This means that these organisations, if considered as part of civil society, have a much closer connection to the State than other organisations. Similarly, educational institutions are largely controlled by the State, so that their role within civil society in China is much weaker than one might expect.[4] This could be problematic, since, if the line between State and civil society becomes too blurred, the ability of civil society to act as force for change becomes diminished. Another contrast to Western conceptions of civil society can be found in Pakistan, where it is observed that many NGOs work in cooperation with the State, providing such services as sanitation in poor quarters of the country. Moreover, during the presidency of Musharraf, many members of Islamic civil society were highly critical of his espousing of Western liberal values. Civil society was willing to forego democratic values in return for modernisation, but rejected the Western liberal values on which they were based (Zaidi, 2008, p. 39). It is evident from just these two examples that conceptions of civil society are rich and varied, displaying a diversity of relationships with the State.

Civil society is contrasted to the State, but is not necessarily opposed to it. The Chinese distinction between gongmín shè huì, people's society, and shì mín shè huì, a narrower, more legal conception referring to townspeople,[5] provides us with an important distinction that enables us to distinguish between civics and civility. Civics is concerned with being a responsible citizen and civility is concerned with being a responsible member of the community. Both rest on individuals possessing underlying moral virtues that ground their actions as citizens and as members of their communities. In the case of being civic-minded, people can be expected to pay their taxes, take an interest in the democratic process of electing those who are to govern, be prepared to support the State during war, obey the law and be generally supportive of the State, for example, by not undermining it through selling its secrets or fomenting revolution. In taking on citizenship of a State, a citizen takes on certain responsibilities. In addition to those for which the individual is responsible to the State, there are also those civic obligations that individuals have to their local communities. This, for example, will mean ensuring that they put their rubbish out to be collected on the designated day, obeying local laws not to litter the park and to respect their neighbours' privacy. None of this need involve very much contact with other persons. Civility, which is a hallmark of a civil society, in contrast, more intimately involves the relationships among individuals and between them and their communities. In order to practise civility, individuals are confronted by other human beings face to face. Civility is marked, therefore, by values and virtues such as respect for persons. A civil society is a moral society because both civics and civility demand that we take account of the needs of others and invite us into relationship with them, however tenuous that relationship might be. Civic society and civil society (the latter understood in the sense of gong mín shè huì) will overlap, since the virtues to be practised in the private sphere are the same ones that are needed in the public sphere, as MacIntyre (1985) argues against liberal views, such as those of Rawls (1972). Although the distinction we have made between civic society and civil society is not always drawn, the nuances of the different Chinese terms for civil society enable us to reflect on different conceptions of civil society, distinguish different features of those conceptions and to show how they are related. The notion of civic society as a form of civil society can be understood to be more closely aligned to the demands of citizenship, rather than membership of a community and so it is to be expected that responsibilities and obligations that membership of the latter entail will be different. Nevertheless, the values and virtues required for civic society will the same as those required for civil society.

In the West, Antonio Gramsci was one of the first to use the term civil society,[6] but he saw it as a means of opposing the status quo and of building a new cultural hegemony, based around the organisation of families, schools, voluntary associations, as well as universities and other institutions, such as the press, that had a degree of influence in the formation of the political values and ideologies of the public. The role of civil society was to oppose the ruling classes, since if revolution was to be effected, civil society would have to be won over first, otherwise the State could not be conquered. Gramsci, however, did not preach militancy in the overthrow of the old order, rather he understood that true revolution is not imposed by force, but is the result of education (Entwistle, 1979, pp. 14–15). Despite his many writings on civil society and hegemony, however, Gramsci does not find a satisfactory account of civil society nor of the State (Hoare, 1971, p. 207). Nevertheless, he enlists the idea of civil society as a means counteracting the State and even though at times he identifies civil society with the State, it is through the direct education of the workers that the hegemony of the bourgeoisie can be overturned and replaced by proletarian hegemony.

The fluidity of Gramsci's views on civil society can be ascribed to the changing views he has on the relationship between State and civil society. This occurs at two levels, since it is not only a matter of changing views through a rethinking of his theoretical position, but also an expression of the ideological struggle that takes place between different forces, resulting in the emergence of a different relationship between civil society and the State. For example, in discussing the theoretical basis of the free trade movement, he notes that a distinction is made between political society (the State) and civil society, so that it is claimed that economic activity belongs to civil society and the State should not interfere by imposing regulations. In this, however, he says that the State and civil society are one and the same and observes that a policy of *laissez faire* in relation to regulation of the market is a deliberate form of policy. He asserts that it is not simply an expression of the free market, but an intentional political programme designed to redistribute national income to the ruling classes (Gramsci, 1971, pp. 159–160). These vested interests have no interest in changing the State or civil society, merely maintaining the status quo. Elsewhere, however, the State is identified with the ruling elite and Gramsci likens the political struggle to a military campaign in which the proletariat seek to seize power for itself. In the West, civil society in this struggle is seen as forming a formidable fortress protecting the State, but separate from it[7] (Gramsci, 1971, p. 238).

These seminal ideas of Gramsci's about civil society can be seen in more recent conceptions of civil society. Gramsci, in considering how power can be shifted to the people, observes that though economic crises can weaken the State and to some extent, bourgeois civil society, they do not necessarily have a lasting effect and warns against the assumption that such events inevitably bring about permanent change (Gramsci, 1971, p. 235). More permanent change demands a change of values and outlook within the whole of civil society. The growth of neoliberalism, it has been argued, has defeated social democracy and so has weakened civil society. This is because the genesis of the Global Financial Crisis (GFC), especially for Europe, is seen as originating in the lack of control of the market, the weakening of democracy and the ascendancy of neoliberalism. The alternative is to control the financial sector, so that it no longer dominates the making of policy. In order to achieve this, however, it will be necessary to develop an alternative narrative about society, one which provides for taxation on financial institutions and a redirection of economic activity to control the flow of capital, protect jobs and wages, and to stimulate demand (Pianta, 2013, pp. 148–156). This, however, fails to take into account Gramsci's observation of the resilience of both State and bourgeois civil society. The result of the GFC has not been a greater regulation of financial markets, but greater austerity, as ordinary taxpayers have been forced to bear the burdens of the debts created by banks and financiers. Habermas contends that Europe is only pretence of democracy, left in the power of financial markets, arguing that the way out is a political integration that could fulfil the promise of the European social model and gives Europe a greater global influence (Habermas, Bofinger, & Nida-Rümelin, 2012). As Gramsci argues political change requires a change in the hegemonic outlook of civil society and is to be accomplished through education.

Gramsci's view that there is a certain degree of fluidity in conceptions of civil society is accepted by Wischermann who prioritises action rather than structure, suggesting that 'civil society is a particular mode of interaction within a given society and not a fixed entity'(Wischermann, 2010, p. 9). Civil society, in this view, implies a set of attitudes that include empathy, respect and willingness to compromise, characterised by 'the existence of a rather high degree of respect vis-a'-vis women and vis-a'-vis various societal and so called marginal groups' (Wischermann, 2010, p. 36). State and civil society, it is proposed, are not separate, but interrelated (Wischermann, 2010, p. 6.). It is subsequently noted that there is an overlap and an interest in civility as a component of a civil society, as we have proposed above (Lewis, 2013, p. 329), the view that civil society is characterised as a mode of interaction between people allows space for many kinds of relationships. In general terms, civil society names the space of uncoerced human association and also the set of relational networks formed for the sake of family, faith, interest and ideology. Civil society means the building of networks of unions, churches, political parties and movements, cooperatives, neighbourhoods, schools of thought, societies for promoting or preventing this and that. (Walzer, 2003, p. 306).

In the discussions surrounding conceptions of civil society, there is a general consensus that civil society stands as a counterweight to the State, to corporations and to the market. Some commentators see it as being represented by various associations that exist between citizens, by NGOs and loosely, by the public sphere. These various associations and organisations can work side by side with governments and with the other public instrumentalities. To some degree, they can also be seen as overlapping with other spheres of activity, such as the State, though whether civil society can overlap with financial institutions and the market seems unlikely. Civil society does not require democracy to exist. Nevertheless, its existence in totalitarian regimes is tenuous because, in such regimes, repression of associations not sanctioned by the State seeks to ensure that there is no dissent and no opposition to the will of the State. This is because free association of individuals may give rise to ideas that the State feels threatened by and so acts to suppress them. Despite this, civil society, especially in the formation of approved associations, can act to support even a totalitarian regime as it mitigates its harshness through the formation of self-help groups, providing welfare services, health services, food, shelter and so on to the most repressed members of the community.[8] In such a form, it can be tolerated by a repressive regime. It is well documented that in totalitarian states, such as in the former Soviet bloc, people find ways in which to circumvent repression and a flourishing underground society can exist.[9] Nevertheless, it is also apparent that decades of repression leave their mark on communities and civil society can be stunted because people do not trust each other and relationships are soured.

Civil society, however, does not have access to power in the way in which the State has and so if its members are to effect any change, they need to use political activism. In a democratic State, citizens have some influence over the political process, but they have little influence over the market or the financial institutions and corporations that exist outside the reach of the political process. In a totalitarian state, there is potentially less ability to influence the political process and possibly even less opportunity to influence financial institutions and corporations.

Taking her lead from Gramsci, Iris Young argues that civil society provides opposition to authoritarian rule. It also enables the emergence of public spheres in which differentiated social sectors express their experience and formulate their opinions. This allows the ordinary citizen to influence the politics of state or corporate institutions or catalyse practical changes within civil society itself (Young, 2000, p. 155). This presupposes that there are democratic processes which allow for change to occur through peaceful means, which may not be the case in the authoritarian regimes she says civil society stands against. Nonetheless, civil society in her account stands as guard against the excesses of State and government.

Three levels of associational life within civil society that are relatively autonomous from state and economy can be distinguished—private association, civic association and political association. Civil society, says Young, refers to the entirety of social life and the relationships between individuals and communities outside state institutions. This suggests that civil society does not overlap with the other two areas, but in fact, there is overlap; it is far better to think of the three areas as involving kinds of activities, rather than being separate spheres (Young, 2000, pp. 157–160). Private associations are activities that people engage in a private capacity, as members of clubs, of religious associations and families. These are characterised by involving only a select number of individuals, such as members of one's club and family. Civic associations, she says, are primarily directed outward from those engaged in them to others. Civic associations aim to serve not only members, but the wider community. For example, civic associations are such organisations as neighbourhood watch, the local environmental society, community arts centre and the like. In principle, civic associations are open to everyone. Political associations focus on what the social collective ought to do. Political associations aim to influence state policy formation or implementation, for example, parties, lobbying organisations and special interest associations organised to influence or protest state policy (Young, 2000, pp. 160–163).

In forming political associations, the oppressed and economically marginalised can seek to redress the injustices from which they suffer, but as the struggle for justice in many places around the world shows, this can be a drawn-out conflict and here Gramsci's metaphor of a military campaign is apt. Nevertheless, there is room for optimism, since it is possible to form self-help groups that can provide services in those areas where the State is unwilling or unable to do so. Some voluntary associations, for example, provide support for immigrants and refugees, women's shelters and youth centres. In some developing countries, these services cannot be provided by the State and so it is up to voluntary associations to undertake these activities that contribute to the common good. Of course some of these may be INGOs and NGOs that operate across borders, as we have already mentioned. Civil society in private and civic associations can provide opportunities for people to connect in different ways, to form experimental groups with special interests, such as, organic farming, herbal healing and evangelical religious worship amongst many others.

Whatever way we characterise civil society, it is apparent that it has the capacity to be a powerful counterbalance and beacon of hope to the oppressed and the marginalised. It exists in uneasy tension with the State. Uneasy, because though at times civil society cooperates with the State, and takes the initiative in areas where the State is falling short, it also can be a site of resistance against it. Sometimes movements begin within civil society and outside the political sphere, but which grow into political forces in their own right. At a fundamental level, civil society involves relationships between people, between people and the State, and between people and the market. These relationships need to be nurtured in their different ways, and education will have a significant role to play in fostering their growth.

**Relationality as an Attribute of Human Nature in East and West**

Civil society, consisting as it does of various clubs, associations and social groups, reveals the importance of human relationships in the fulfilment of human persons. Human identity can only be properly revealed in the relationships and interactions that human beings have with each other. Both in Western and Eastern accounts of what it is to be a human being, human sociability is identified as a key feature. We cannot be who we are without others. We cannot hope to foster the associations which are a feature of civil society if we have not cultivated our capacity to relate to one another, to learn cooperation and to understand that to be fully human is to be responsible for the other. We have identified this cultivation as an aim of education.

In the *Politics*, Aristotle asserts that human beings are social animals:

> Man is by nature a social animal; an individual who is unsocial naturally and not accidentally is either beneath our notice or more than human. Society is something that precedes the individual. Anyone who either cannot lead the common life or is so self-sufficient as not to need to, and therefore does not partake of society, is either a beast or a god.[10] (Aristotle, 1981, Book I, Ch. II [1253a])

Later, in the same passage, when considering the origins of the State, Aristotle notes that the State in order of time follows that of the individual, but in the order of nature, is prior to the individual. What Aristotle means is that no human being can exist properly fulfilled without the help of the family and the State. When separated from others, human beings are either gods or beasts. Without law and justice, human beings cannot become the fully human persons that they can be, and so they remain at the level of animals. Moreover, society is to the individual as the whole is to a part, and so it is society or State which is the greater, since the good to which the whole aims is greater than the good to which the individual aims.

Aquinas, in the prologue to his Commentary on *The Politics*, notes that human beings form associations, but that the greatest of these is the political association because it is directed to what is self-sufficient for human life (2007, p. 2). There is,

Aquinas notes, a variety of associations that human beings form, such as families, larger households, states and these are not simply larger versions of the same thing, but insists that these are constituted by very different relationships between the members of each of these; it is not simply a matter of larger numbers. The head of a family, for example, will have a very different relationship with its members than a king with his subjects (2007, p. 4). Similarly, the government of a nation will have a different relationship with its citizens and as we have argued, civil society because it is composed of a variety of associations, will have a diverse range of relationships with its members. All of these, especially civil society, will have an influence on forming the identities and characters of human persons.

Confucian philosophy has a very clear understanding of the connection between a person's community and its role in forming the individual's identity because it acknowledges that we cannot be ourselves without the other. Individual identity exists in relationship with the community to which the individual belongs. In naming an individual it is not his or her individual name that comes first, but his or her family name. Thus, a Chinese name, such as 邬 益芳, Wū Yì Fāng, does not begin, as in the Western world, with the person's first name, but with his or her family name, since it is this which specifies the familial community to which he or she belongs and places the person within a network of relationships. Each person has his or her place within a hierarchy of relationships and this establishes the responsibilities and obligations of each person. Knowing one's place leads to social harmony. Relations with others is the key to understanding the nature of the human being, since it is through belonging to a community, initially the family, that identity as a human being is established. The virtue of rén, 仁, love of self and love of others, also rendered benevolence or humaneness, reinforces the notion that to develop as human beings, which is to say as moral beings, we cannot do without other people. Confucius says that the person of virtue will give up his or her life in order to preserve virtue, which means that our lives are fulfilled through our relationships of love with others and we should never act to jeopardise those loving relationships.[11] The importance of our relationships with others can also be observed through the development of the virtue of lǐ, 礼, propriety, which demands that the individual, both publicly and privately observes the right kind of behaviour required by particular circumstances. Hence, if the situation demands expressing condolences, then the practice of lǐ ensures that we perform the right rituals in the right circumstances. While the observance of ritual propriety lǐ is important, it is not enough. This is because we have to respond to the other person in the right kind of way, with humaneness and with empathy.[12] In order to respond to the other in the right kind of way, virtue has to be cultivated and this is the preeminent task of education. The basic elements of Confucian education are designed to develop character that is to be formed through self-cultivation (xiū shēn 修身) and the development of propriety (lǐ (礼)) and benevolence, or humaneness (rén, 仁). This, however, takes place within a hierarchy of relationships and cultivation of the virtues, and, because it involves living in harmony with others, cannot be divorced from the community to which persons belong.

In understanding that we are for others and formed by them, it will be by our fundamental evaluations, Taylor argues, that who we are as persons is defined; it is not given by any list of properties such as my physical description, where I came from, or background capacities. These can have some role to play in describing us, but what are more significant are our strong evaluations, that is, what we value as important. These evaluations shape the relationships that we have with others and in turn shape who we are. Thus, our ancestry, of coming from a certain lineage, or of coming from a certain ethnic background will be an important component of how we see ourselves if our evaluation of such distinguishing characteristics is highly valued by us (Taylor, 1985, p. 34). Some of these evaluations, however, will not be entirely of our own choosing: I cannot choose not to be of a certain ethnic origin even if I deny that origin, or don't see it as having importance. It is this fundamental incarnational aspect of who we are that we have no control over. In the denial of our origins, we attempt to deny that we belong to a particular community and there is a denial of our own identity and character. We seek to cut ourselves off from the community to which we belong, sometimes to forge a new identity. This is a strong evaluation and this will affect how we describe ourselves, but it also means that we need to identify ourselves with another community. We cannot escape relationality.

Relationality, central to the formation of human persons and the creation of the just society, is nurtured in families and cultivated in civil society. The challenge is to provide the institutions that will enable that formation. While much of this formation takes place informally within families and in local communities, it cannot be entirely left to them. They will not have the resources to accomplish the formation of persons in the virtues and values that they need to become active participants in the creation of a just society. Educational institutions, schools and universities, have traditionally been entrusted with this task, but their focus, under the sway of neoliberalism, on those aspects of education that produce measureable outcomes has meant that the educational aim of fostering the growth of virtue in persons, so that they can take their place in the critical transformation of their societies has been neglected. This is not surprising, since a preoccupation with quantification of outcomes in education has led to a concentration on what is thought to be measureable. The question of what is measureable and whether it is important to measure it, however, is complex. In particular, measurement of any kind is fraught with problems in the educational context. There is no straightforwardly reliable means of measuring how well we have succeeded in cultivating virtuous, authentic persons with a commitment to the creation of a just society. This leads us to propose, as have many others, that the emphasis on quantitative measurement in education obscures the importance of what cannot be measured. We argue that a recognition of limitations of measurement will bring into view the relative unimportance of what can be measured and will enable us to focus on the formation of human persons and their relationships with others in order to build a civil society that is just and seeks the common good.

## Measurement and Educational Aims

In a speech to the University of Kansas, Lawrence, Kansas in 1968, Robert Kennedy encapsulated the problem of trying to measure everything, but failing to pay heed to what is important. He observed:

> Too much and too long, we seem to have surrendered community excellence and community values in the mere accumulation of material things. ... Gross National Product does not include the beauty of our poetry or the intelligence of our public debate; measures neither our wit nor our courage, neither our wisdom nor our learning, neither our compassion nor our devotion to our country; it measures everything, in short, except that which makes life worthwhile.[13]

The point Kennedy makes highlights the problem with placing too much reliance on what can be quantified through numerical measurement. The accumulation of wealth can be measured and is mistaken for success, the accumulation of high scores in examinations and entry into prestigious courses and institutions is taken as success, but as Kennedy says, those things which make life worthwhile fail to fit the measurement paradigm and so are neglected by governments and educational institutions alike. Commitment to civil society, to justice and the common good, for example, though it can be recognised and applauded in an individual is not quantifiable, since its effects cannot be measured and moreover can wax and wane overtime.

The focus by governments on measurement in education is partly due to the corrupting influence of the intrusion of the economic sphere into education. What is symptomatic of this intrusion is the attempt to quantify everything that occurs within an educational context, ignoring what cannot be quantified in any straightforward way. The result of this is that education becomes narrowly focussed on what is measureable. As Hardie (1978) points out, certain kinds of fundamental measurements cannot be undertaken in education. This does not mean that no measurement can be undertaken, but it raises the questions of what can be measured and what the measurement is meant to represent. It is contended that much of what is important in education cannot be measured but educators in both East and West are beguiled by measurements of various kinds because these appear to validate claims of educational achievement. This means that they concentrate on what is measureable to the detriment of what we claim are the central concerns of education.

What is measureable is performance. That is, assessments of skills and capacities that students have developed in the course of study. Achievement in educational circles has had a different meaning to performance. It has been widely used to mean mastery of a subject or completion of a task.[14] Peters (1966, p. 26) takes the view that achievement has a broader sense in educational contexts and is applicable to a wider range of activities, not just measureable performances. It also means that something worthwhile has been imparted, including general virtues, such as a sense of relevance, precision, the power to concentrate as well as such moral virtues as courage and sensitivity to others. Most, if not all, of these virtues that Peters mentions will not be measureable. Achievement defined as an overall performance measure as a result leaves out what Robert Kennedy described as what is most worthwhile for human beings. It is hard to escape the conclusion that what is most important as an aim in education is not able to be measured at all.

Even where measurement of achievement is possible, it is clear that quantification is only possible in limited ways. Though the assessment of what students have accomplished during their study is important, the limitations of assessment mean that those elements of education crucial to the development of the civil society and in the formation of good persons escape any attempt at assessment because they cannot be measured. As a result, they are ignored either as an unimportant part of education or because they are not measureable, that they are meaningless, just as positivism holds. As a result, much of what is worthwhile about life—and education—has little place in the institutions charged with the formation of human persons and the development of civil society.[15]

## Conclusion

We began with the claim that various events around the globe have emphasised the yearning of many people for justice and for the freedom to lead fulfilled lives with their families. We argued that for people to be able to realise their yearnings, it was incumbent on communities to foster a civil society. A crucial question, however, was to provide some account of the nature of civil society. Though the concept could be described as contested, it could be seen as standing as a counterweight to the State and to the market. More than this, as Gramsci argued, it was central to the transformation of society through the fostering of social justice and the common good. Gramsci saw education as fundamental in the development of persons who could act to alleviate poverty, suffering and oppression. The same impulse to develop a just and fair society is also at the heart of Confucianism. Desire for justice and for the common good is the same for communities in both East and West. Education, it was concluded, had a crucial role in the development of a civil society, but it was not clear whether it measured up. In conceptions of Education influenced by the market economy, it was argued, the focus on measureable outcomes meant that only what could be measured or counted was recognised as worthwhile. As a result, educational institutions are ill-equipped to contribute to the fostering of civil society, humane government and an economic sector that is concerned with the common good, rather than just profits.

The most significant feature in civil society is its role in the formation of the identity of human persons and this is because the distinctiveness and uniqueness of each individual could only be understood in relation to others. Relationality is important in both Eastern and Western understanding of the development of the human person. Human beings need education in order for them to develop their ability to relate to others and to cultivate the virtues needed to be good and humane persons. These virtues and attributes are crucial elements in the development of a just, harmonious and humane civil society. Human beings and civil society are interrelated: civil society consists of human beings in relationship and so the quality of civil society will depend on the qualities of its members.

If the key undertaking of education is the development of persons to be good and humane individuals and by extension, the nurturing of the civil society, then it seems that if it achieves this at all it is by default. Educational institutions, forced by governments to be constantly justifying what they do by demonstrating that they quantifiably measure up to the goals set by government, are failing in their broader educative responsibilities. It is because of the focus on these externally imposed goals that the broader educative aims of developing civil society and forming human beings is almost invisible in the education systems of East and West. At least another one of the reasons for this is because the achievement of these broader goals is not easily measureable, if at all. The task that we face as educators is to find a way to loosen the grip of the positivist thought that only what can be measureable is real and that the rest, because it cannot be measured is unreal and so not a proper subject for education to concern itself with. This is the challenge that educators need to tackle in both East and West and it is something which needs to start in their classrooms.

## Disclosure statement

No potential conflict of interest was reported by the author.

## Notes

1. Said to have begun in Tunisia in December 2010 and followed by uprisings across the Arab world. See Dabashi (2012) for discussion of the Arab Spring.
2. By human identity, we mean what it is to be a human being. This would require an account of human anthropology. By personal identity, we mean those attributes that contribute to our recognition of ourselves as individuals.
3. INGOs include such organisations as the Red Cross, Amnesty International, Médecins Sans Frontiers, Greenpeace and Caritas.
4. There is some controversy about the extent to which education is considered to be controlled by the State in China. Considered as a relatively autonomous institution in civil society it could be a means of addressing some of the ills of society, alternatively, if it is a creature of the State, it could be seen as simply furthering the interests of the State. Because of factions within the government, however, educational policy is not always consistent and this leaves some room for independence (Tsang, 2000, pp. 581–582).
5. Gōngmín shè huì, 公民社会, literally translated means citizen's society or community, while shì mín shè huì, 市民 社会, means city residents' society. The second is more formal, since it implies some kind of civic obligation. Mínjiān shè huì, 民间社会, literally means among the people society and so could be understood to stand for NGOs, amongst other kinds of associations.
6. The concept of civil society is not new and appears in Hegel's *Philosophy of Right*. See Hegel (1991).
7. Gramsci, as already noted, is sometimes not clear on the distinctions between State and civil society. This is because the State is sometimes identified with the ruling class and civil society with the proletariat, but in fact, the bourgeoisie also form civil society. In one sense, the State is supported by the civil society of the bourgeoisie and so they form a unity, in another sense, if civil society stands against the State, then it is identified with the proletariat. The reality is that bourgeoisie and proletariat could be considered as forming civil society together.
8. Lewis reports that civic associations can adopt some of the aspects of the totalitarian regimes in which they operate. They are able to flourish because some of their goals accord with those of the regime. See Lewis (2013, p. 328). The ethical dilemma here is that by cooperating with the totalitarian regime they may be assisting in the oppression of the people who they are trying to help.
9. Iris Young says, 'However despised or disenfranchised, in a liberal society (and even sometimes in illiberal societies) people who are disadvantaged or marginalised can find each

other and form associations to improve their lives through mutual aid and articulation of group consciousness' (Young, 2000, p. 165).
10. The Jowett translation of the *Politics* says man is by nature a political animal, but the sense of what is said by Aristotle in the passage refers to the idea of the human being as a social being.
11. Kongzi (Confucius) says that the determined scholar and the man of virtue will not seek to live at the expense of injuring their virtue. They will even sacrifice their lives to preserve their virtue complete. (子曰、志士、仁人、無求生以害仁、有殺身以成仁) Confucius (1971) *The Analects*, 15.8. Elsewhere, he notes the importance of relationships and says that virtue is not left to stand alone. He who practises it will have neighbours. (子曰、德不孤、必有鄰) Confucius (1971) *The Analects*, 4.25.
12. Kongzi says, 'In the ceremonies of mourning, it is better that there be deep sorrow than in minute attention to observances'. (寧儉、喪、與其易也、寧戚) Confucius (1971) *The Analects*, 3.4.
13. A fuller extract of Robert Kennedy's is worth reading 'Too much and too long, we seem to have surrendered community excellence and community values in the mere accumulation of material things. Our gross national product ... if we should judge America by that - counts air pollution and cigarette advertising, and ambulances to clear our highways of carnage. It counts special locks for our doors and the goals for those who break them. It counts the destruction of our redwoods and the loss of our natural wonder in chaotic sprawl. It counts napalm and the cost of a nuclear warhead, and armoured cars for police who fight riots in our streets. It counts Whitman's rifle and Speck's knife, and the television programmes which glorify violence in order to sell toys to our children. Yet the gross national product does not allow for the health of our children, the quality of their education, or the joy of their play. It does not include the beauty of our poetry or the strength of our marriages; the intelligence of our public debate or the integrity of our public officials. It measures neither our wit nor our courage; neither our wisdom nor our learning; neither our compassion nor our devotion to our country; it measures everything, in short, except that which makes life worthwhile. And it tells us everything about America except why we are proud that we are Americans'. Address to the University of Kansas, Lawrence, Kansas, March 18, 1968.
14. The task and achievement dichotomy was discussed by Ryle (1949) in his very influential text, *the Concept of Mind*. Task words are such words as 'hunting', since they denote engagement in an activity, while achievement words are words such as 'finding' (Ryle, 1949, pp. 149–153).
15. It is noteworthy that attempts have been made to measure aspects of civil society. Anheier (2004) provides an account of how some aspects of civil society may be measured. He acknowledges the immense difficulty of the task.

# References

Anheier, H. K. (2004). *Civil society: Measurement, evaluation, policy*. London: Earthscan.

Aquinas T. (2007). *Commentary on Aristotle's politics* (R. J. Regan, Trans.). Indianapolis: Hackett.
Aristotle. (1976). *The Nichomachean ethics* (J. A. K. Thomson, Trans., intro. and bibliography J. Barnes, rev. ed. with notes and appendices Hugh Tredinnick). Harmondsworth: Penguin.
Aristotle. (1981). *The politics* (Rev. ed., T. A. Sinclair, Trans., T. J. Saunders, Rev and re-presented). London: Penguin.
Confucius. (1971). *Confucius: Confucian analects, the great learning and the doctrine of the mean* (J. Legge, Trans.). London: Dover (Originally published 1893, Oxford: Clarendon Press).
Dabashi, H. (2012). *The Arab spring: The end of post-colonialism.* London: Zed Books.
Entwistle, H. (1979). *Antonio Gramsci: Conservative schooling for radical politics.* London: Routledge and Kegan Paul.
Evans, P. (2000). Fighting marginalization with transnational networks: Counter-hegemonic globalization. *Contemporary Sociology, 29*, 230–241.
Gramsci, A. (1971). *Selections from the prison notebooks of Antonio Gramsci* (Q. Hoare & G. Nowell-Smith, Eds. and Trans.). New York, NY: International Publishers.
Habermas, J., Bofinger, P., & Nida-Rümelin, J. (2012, August 4). *Il Passo Decisivo Per Salvare l' Europa* [The decisive step to save Europe]. p. 1. Retrieved from http://ricerca.repubblica.it/repubblica/archivio/repubblica/2012/08/04/il-passo-decisivo-per-salvare-leuropa.html?ref=search
Hardie, C. D. (1978). Measurement in education. *Educational Theory, 28*, 54–61.
Hegel, G. F. W. (1991). *Elements of the philosophy of right* (A. W. Wood, Ed. & H. B. Nisbet, Trans.). Cambridge: Cambridge University Press.
Hoare, G. (1971). Introduction. In A. Gramsci (1971). *Selections from the prison notebooks of Antonio Gramsci* (Q. Hoare & G. Nowell-Smith, Eds. Trans.) (pp. 206–209). New York, NY: International Publishers.
Kennedy, R. F. (1968). *Address to the University of Kansas, Lawrence, Kansas, March 18, 1968.* Retrieved from http://images2.americanprogress.org/campus/email/RobertFKennedyUniversityofKansas.pdf
Keping, Y., Thornton, J. L., & Li, C. (2009). *Democracy is a good thing : Essays on politics, society, and culture in contemporary China.* Washington, DC: Brookings Institution Press.
Kingsnorth, P. (2003). *One no, many yeses: A journey to the heat of the global resistance movement.* London: The Free Press.
Lewis, D. (2013). Civil society and the authoritarian state: Cooperation, contestation and discourse. *Journal of Civil Society, 9*, 325–340.
MacIntyre, A. (1985). *After virtue: A study in moral theory* (2nd ed.). London: Duckworth.
Mencius, M. (1970). *Mencius* (D. C. Lau, Trans.). Harmondsworth: Penguin.
Milner, H. (2003). Civic literacy in global civil society: Excluding the majority from democratic participation. In G. Laxer & S. Halperin (Eds.), *Global civil society and its limits* (pp. 189–209). Basingstoke: Palgrave Macmillan.
Peters, R. S. (1966). *Ethics and education.* London: George Allen and Unwin.
Pianta, M. (2013). Democracy lost: The financial crisis in Europe and the role of civil society. *Journal of Civil Society, 9*, 148–161.
Rawls, J. (1972). *A theory of justice.* Oxford: Clarendon Press.
Ryle, G. (1949). *The concept of mind.* London: Hutchinson.
Taylor, C. (1985). *Human agency and language* (Vol. 1). Cambridge: Cambridge University Press.
Taylor, R. (Ed.). (2004). *Creating a better world: Interpreting global civil society.* Bloomfield, CT: Kumarian Press.
Tsang, M. (2000). Education and national development in China since 1949: Oscillating policies and enduring dilemmas. In L. C. Ming & J. Shen (Eds.), *China Review 2000* (pp. 579–618). Hong Kong: The Chinese University Press.

Walzer, M. (2003). A better vision: The idea of civil society. In V. A. Hodgkinson & M. W. Foley (Eds.), *The civil society reader* (pp. 306–321). Hanover, NH: Tufts University Press.
Waterman, P. (1996). Beyond globalism and developmentalism: Other voices in world politics. *Development and Change, 27*, 165–180.
Wischermann, J. (2010). Civil society action and governance in Vietnam: Selected findings from an empirical survey. *Journal of Current Southeast Asian Affairs, 29*, 3–40.
Young, I. M. (2000). *Inclusion and democracy*. Oxford: Oxford University Press.
Zaidi, S. A. (2008). An emerging civil society? *Journal of Democracy, 19*, 38–40.

# Can Educationally Significant Learning be Assessed?

STEVEN A. STOLZ

**Abstract**

*This article argues that assessment is a central feature of teaching, particularly as a means to determine whether what has been taught has been learnt. However, I take issue with the current trend in education which places a significant amount of emphasis upon large-scale public testing, which in turn has exacerbated the 'teaching-to-the-test' syndrome, not to mention distorting teaching decisions that are detrimental to the overall development of student knowledge and understanding. Part of the problem with assessment in education seems to revolve around the nature of knowledge and how best to assess human knowledge and understanding. Although much philosophical uncertainty and disagreement exists surrounding the nature of knowledge, I argue that coming to know something is a* sine qua non *of any education. In saying this, I highlight the limits of assessment by demonstrating how certain activities are resistant to large-scale public testing because they are not easily reducible to facts which can be tested for, or at least in the same way as propositional forms of knowledge. Consequently, my argument is a philosophical one to the effect that assessment, particularly large-scale public testing is incapable of assessing all forms of learning, or even the quality of student understanding because the instruments available are both too blunt and tend to capture a certain kind of knowledge that privileges theory over practice, and mental skills over physical skills.*

**Introduction**

Assessment is an inevitable part of education. Indeed teacher assessment is an extension of the close relationship between teaching and learning. For instance, it is not uncommon for teachers to utilise a range of assessment instruments as a mechanism to ascertain whether what has been taught has been achieved by students. Certainly, those teachers who are serious about their teaching will be concerned about whether their planned for activities have been effective in bringing about learning, particularly the extent to which they are successful or not. Of course, the interest in assessing learning is nothing new and can be traced as far back as Plato.[1] However, a particular concern I have at the moment surrounds the trend in educational discourse which places a significant amount of emphasis upon large-scale public testing that reduces education to something very narrow, such performance in tests as a means to ascertain certain types of knowledge which fails to capture human *understanding* of deeper learning. For instance, under neoliberal regimes, there is an attempt to control the curriculum and outcomes of education using testing as the controlling mechanism. An obvious example is the National Assessment Programme—Literacy and Numeracy (NAPLAN) annual assessment of Years 3, 5, 7 and 9 students across the whole of Australia.[2] A central feature of NAPLAN is the publication of individual school performance results on the 'My School' website (see e.g. www.myschool.edu.au). It is interesting to note that the My School website has the capacity to compare the results of one school against another in the same geographical area. The intent of NAPLAN and the My School website is to raise standards, but it also implicitly recognises that schools and teachers should be held publically accountable for these standards. Taking into consideration, the late twentieth-century neoliberal occupation with global competitiveness education would appear to have also become essentially subservient to assessing performance in order to fulfil some pre-defined vocational or socio-economic useful ends. There is a strong sense that funds allocated to various educational systems should be accountable to the taxpayer for equipping children and young people with certain fundamental skills like numeracy and literacy in an economically efficient way. In a neoliberal climate, these skills are seen as a necessary pre-requisite for students who will eventually enter the workforce and contribute in some way to increased economic competitiveness and economically exploitable skills commonly known as 'human capital'. Central to this commercial paradigm in educational discourse is the role of the market in providing 'buyers with information about the relationship between the quality and the price of goods' (Winch, 1996b, p. 97). The argument goes, since the taxpayer provides the financial resources to schools in order to provide a quality educational product for 'customers of education', then the education provided needs to be accounted for to the customer (or taxpayer) in order to demonstrate value for money and quality service (Winch, 1996b). Subsequently, large-scale public testing such as NAPLAN and the reporting of these results on the My School website are obvious examples of the influence of neoliberal point of view of accountability between efficient resource provision and quality education.

Although writing from a United Kingdom perspective, Davis (1995, 1996) raises an important point surrounding large-scale public testing and the tendency of teachers to distort their teaching decisions which tend to result in the familiar 'teaching-to-the-test' syndrome.[3] The obvious concern here being that 'teaching-to-the-test' is detrimental to the overall development of student knowledge and understanding, not to mention potentially corrupting.[4] Other concerns surrounding assessment policy range from confusing educational standards with improving test performance, the unjust use of assessment to hold schools and teachers to account for students learning, teachers being told how to teach and still being held accountable for students learning, an inability to accurately judge what is considered to be quality teaching (see e.g. Davis, 1999). Winch and Gingell (1996) in their reply to Davis (1995) draw attention to how the main argument against assessment is a epistemological one that 'urges a form of scepticism about whether it is possible to know that anyone has learned anything' (p. 380). Likewise, Winch (1996a) in discussing the notion of how 'quality' is manufactured in educational systems highlights how certain instruments are used to monitor systems at a macro- or micro-level within an institution. This means that the choice of instrument to verify quality assurance, to some extent is a political one because the data collected are often used to generate reports for public dissemination as a means to increase market share and/or accountability to its users (or purchasers). In the latter case, quality is judged according to whether the educational product meets their needs and wants. Clearly, there is a significant disconnect between short-term user satisfaction as a criterion of success and the long-term aims of education that seek to *change* their students rather than influence them to come back and purchase the educational product again. In saying this, large-scale public testing is just one mechanism amongst many to assure quality control in educational systems. Part of the problem is that there has been a general misconstrual that there is a direct causal connection between the quality of teaching and student outcomes in large-scale public tests. For instance, NAPLAN assumes that there is a connection between teaching performance and student learning because the My School website provides the various assessment data on a school by school basis and hence possible to compare schools according to geography. Not only does this highlight a rather narrow conception of education, but more importantly, it neglects the fact that there are significant limits to what assessment—particularly large-scale public tests—can tell us both about the quality of student understanding and what the student has learned. Consequently, for the purposes of this article, I will be concerned with the critical discussion of two issues: first, I briefly outline how the Platonic view of knowledge has influenced educational epistemology to conclude that knowledge and understanding can be assessed. In turn, this has led to much philosophical controversy and disagreement about the role of knowledge in education, and lastly, I answer my own self-imposed question: Can educationally significant learning be assessed? The conclusion towards which I argue is that some educational aims can easily be assessed (assuming that the tests are valid and reliable), such as low-level tests of numeracy and literacy, however, my argument is a philosophical one to the effect that assessment, particularly large-scale public testing is incapable of assessing all forms of learning, or even the quality of student understanding because the instruments available are both too blunt and tend to capture a certain kind of knowledge that privileges theory over practice, and mental skills over physical skills.

**Knowledge and Education: The Influence of Plato and the Problem of Objectivity**

The best point of entry into this debate surrounding knowledge and education is clearly provided by the sophists. Plato in *Theaetetus* offers a philosophical account of the nature of knowledge, which is often recognised as a piercing critique on what it means to know something is true (or false), and hence assessable as true according to certain necessary conditions. Socrates starts out by rejecting Theaetetus' view that knowledge is 'nothing but sense perception' (Plato, 1961, *Theaetetus*, 151e). In order to refute Theaetetus' claims, Socrates highlights how Protagoras shared the same view when he stated that 'man is the measure of all things' (*Theaetetus*, 152a). He goes on to add that the problem with the senses is that they have the potential to deceive us to the point that what I may perceive or experience to be hot or red, you may perceive or experience as cold or blue. Although, I can believe whatever I like, this does not make it verifiably true or even knowledge in the strict sense because individual perception can easily fall foul to 'false perceptions' which leads the individual to believe something to be true or real when it may be false or imaginary. Even though it may be possible to believe what I like such as 'Socrates is Theaetetus or Theaetetus Socrates', such beliefs do not equate to knowledge because one can only have knowledge of what is true (*Theaetetus*, 188b). This is reinforced by Socrates when he argues that 'surely a man does not imagine that things he does know are things he does not know, or that things he does not know are things he knows?' (*Theaetetus*, 188b). Certainly, it is possible to become mistaken about something one did not know beforehand or in something that was believed to be true; however, this does not count as knowledge. Even though belief may be true, it is only contingently truth until there are rational grounds or evidence for the truth of these claims. In Socrates words (*Theaetetus*, 196a):

> Well now, does a man ever consider in his mind five and seven—I don't mean five and seven men or anything of that sort, but just five and seven themselves, which we describe as records in that waxen block of ours, among which there can be no false judgement—does anyone ever take these into consideration and ask himself in his inward conversation how much they amount to, and does one man believe and state that they make eleven, another that they make twelve, or does everybody agree they make twelve?

Here, we start to see a sharp distinction between facts, information, beliefs and so on. Of course it cannot possibly be true that 5 and 7 men amount to 11 men, and to argue otherwise would be an error or false judgement because 5 and 7 men is *a priori* 'knowable' as 11 and verifiable as such by others. It is not until Socrates introduces the crucial condition of knowledge which he calls a *'logos'* ('λόγος') that anything or everything that might count as rational or intelligible can have any meaning. According to Carr (2003a), Plato's 'enduring epistemological legacy' is his analysis of knowledge as subject to three constraints: (1) an agent who claims to know $p$ must also believe $p$, which he refers to as the 'psychological constraint'; (2) $p$ must be true, which he calls the 'truth constraint', and; (3) an agent must have grounds or evidence for holding that $p$, which he calls the 'evidence constraint' (pp. 119–120). The Platonic conditions of knowledge clearly influenced many past and present philosophers of education. Indeed, Peters (1966) is often regarded as the catalyst for the diverse array of literature on knowledge and curriculum that followed in the 1960s and 1970s, but it was his colleague P. H. Hirst who was to make the greater impact in terms of general educational epistemology. Hirst's (1965, 1973, 1974) chapter titled, 'Liberal education and the nature of knowledge' which featured his concept of the 'forms of knowledge' doctrine had a tremendous influence not only on educational thinking about knowledge and understanding in Britain, but in most English language-speaking countries around the world. Despite widespread consensus within educational circles that coming to know something is a central tenet of what it means to be educated, some educational philosophers have come to question whether the pursuit of knowledge should be the only aim of education, particularly in relation to the types of knowledge that should be transmitted and whether this is a suitable aim for all student learners. Indeed, the common complaint is that knowledge is often equated with coming to know useless factoids or information which may albeit serve the purposes of assessment within schools, but have no applicability outside it.

According to Carr (1998, 2003a, 2003b, 2010), by the mid-1970s to the 1980s, the value of educational epistemology came to be questioned by so-called postmodern and poststructuralist critiques of thought in education. Indeed, this movement surrounding what it means to *know* something raised a number of fundamental questions about the role of epistemology in education, particularly in relation to objective knowledge and truth. For instance, if the prime purpose of education is the initiation of students into rational forms of knowledge and understanding this leaves little place in the curriculum for subjects and skills that do not obviously meet this criteria like physical education, dance and so on. Understandably, the focus on non-instrumental thinking surrounding education and schooling was criticised as privileging certain forms of knowledge and exalting the intellectual or academic over the practical and useful. Central to the contestability of knowledge concerns the understanding of objective truth upon which to base our knowledge claims, particularly when there are rival narratives or truth claims. MacIntyre, for example, views the notion of truth (or 'good') as a synthesis of rival traditions within a socially established practice in which the *ends* (telos) have been agreed upon by the community (see e.g. MacIntyre, 1981/2007, 1988, 1990, 1999; Stolz, 2015b).[5] From the Platonic view of knowledge, mathematical propositions of the form $2 + 3 = 5$ are true today, in 30 years time and in any part of the universe. On the face of it, this seems reasonable and straight forward, but non-realist or idealist critiques would argue that there is no such thing as objective truth to base knowledge upon because such claims are essentially expressions of cultural and social conventions. The argument goes, since mathematics is a social construction of a system of rules and principles, mathematical claims of the form $2 + 3 = 5$ can only be true by virtue of their place within the system of mathematical rules and principles, and hence, truth is only relative to a system. From this viewpoint, knowledge is relative and contingent upon how knowledge is explained or understood. In saying this, the basic problem of grounding knowledge in Plato's epistemology is a desire to demonstrate that knowledge is objective truth that is equated with certainty that is rationally verifiable, rather than mere assertion, subjective perception and/or belief. In a sense, Plato's epistemology has been the catalyst for assessment that attempts to capture student learning of so-called objective knowledge.

Due to advancements in empirical–psychological instruments, some educational aims are relatively easy to measure (assuming that the tests are valid and reliable), such as low-level tests of numeracy and literacy. Of course, it is a self-evident truism that assessment has a role to play in education; however, I am not too sure we have considered all the limits of assessment and whether educationally significant learning can be assessed and measured in quasi-scientific forms that we so desire because the instruments available are both too blunt and tend to capture a certain kind of knowledge that privileges theory over practice, and mental skills over physical skills. Consequently, in the next section, I answer my self-imposed question: Can educationally significant learning be assessed?

## On the Limits of Assessment: Can Educationally Significant Learning be Assessed?

A sound understanding of the close relationship between teaching and learning is zcrucial because much conceptual confusion exists. The notion that teaching is directed towards the achievement of learning is significant because it highlights the close relationship between teaching and learning. Since a large amount of what we understand about learning in education owes much to the enormous influence of twentieth-century psychology, it needs to be noted from the outset that educationally significant learning can take many different forms and that sometimes people come to understand in surprising ways that do not fit neatly within empirical or rationalist explanations of learning (see e.g. Stolz, 2015a). On the notion of 'educationally significant learning', Oakeshott (1967, p. 156) said it well when he argued that:

> Learning is the comprehensive activity in which we come to know ourselves and the world around us. It is a paradoxical activity: it is doing and submitting at the same time. And its achievements range from merely being aware, to what may be called understanding and being able to explain.

Unfortunately, the relationship between teaching and learning has become misconstrued, and to the point that teaching is often regarded as an applied science or technology in which the end product is apt for assessing (Carr, 2000, 2001, 2003a; Gipps, 1994). The argument goes that effective teachers possess certain characterisable skills or techniques in a type of causal chain of actual or potential behaviour which can be acquired for producing students with the desired outcome of good results (see e.g. Carr, 2000). In this case, the whole process would appear to be causally constructed via a 'technology of pedagogy' that is grounded in an empirical science of learning (Carr, 2003a). A central figure in the scientific or technical approach to teaching was Skinner (1968). He argued that the learning process was measurable either through observable behaviour change or by examination of the content or knowledge taught. The influence of Skinners behaviourism was to have a lasting legacy in education which has gone on to spawn a diverse array of empirically or experimentally conceived research surrounding educational practice. Here, we start to see the scientific or technical approach to teaching which fallaciously perceives a causal type relationship between teaching and learning. For instance, if the teacher taught X, the best way to ascertain whether the student or students have in fact successfully learnt X is to test for this knowledge with an appropriate assessment instrument. The assumption being that if the teaching of X was effective, then the student or students should be able to successfully and satisfactory demonstrate what they know about X, and the assessment instrument should be able to measure the quality of this student understanding and learning. Indeed, we should heed more closely what Hirst (1971) has to say about the close conceptual relationship between teaching and learning when he clearly pre-empted this, and warned that it is '... *not* the case that teaching necessarily implies learning' (p. 10). Although, teaching can facilitate learning, we should not lose sight that there is no logical implication that it will cause learning because education is more complex than this. Likewise, I would like to refute once and for all the inference made by NAPLAN that there a causal relationship between teaching and learning. This is further reinforced by Jarvis (2006) and Moore (2004, 2012) who quite rightly argues that there is no direct evidence to indicate that the teaching process can be accurately assessed in the way some teaching authorities and governments would like it to be due to the complex nature of teaching and learning. Consequently, NAPLAN seeks to assess what students have learnt, however, to assert that this also measures the effectiveness of teaching—since good teaching is claimed to be causally linked to efficacious learning—fails miserably to provide an account of the processes by which students come to understand or make sense of something in a meaningful way (Carr, 1992, 1994, 2003a).[6]

I have no quarrel with some forms formative or summative assessment in order to closely monitor learner understanding of what is being taught. What I do take issue with, however, is assessment that tends to disproportionately focus on propositional forms of knowledge and at the same time neglects or distorts other forms of knowledge such as practical knowledge.[7] Certainly, part of the problem why practical knowledge is not sufficiently understood is due to the fallacious claim that this form of learning is a dressed-up form of behaviourism that is devoid of cognition (see e.g. Stolz, 2013). Likewise, I take issue with the trend in educational discourse which gives greater priority to large-scale public testing as a measure of comparative quality of education between schools (see e.g. My School website that is linked with NAPLAN results). In this latter case, my main concern is that large-scale public testing is incapable of assessing all forms of learning (only some) because it can only assess limited kinds of learning, even in those areas where it is thought that it is possible to assess significant learning, such as in literacy and numeracy. Similarly, the quality of student understanding which Davis (1995, 1996) refers to as 'rich knowledge and understanding', not to mention the difficulties surrounding any set of assessment instruments which are both 'valid and reliable' to assess this understanding. To Davis (1995, pp. 6–7), 'rich knowledge' requires the existence of:

> ... rich beliefs, which, when true and held with justification and understanding ... will be interconnected in a complex network ... which are connected in appropriate ways, and the owner of the beliefs having an appreciation of these 'connections'.

Central to Davis' understanding of rich knowledge contrasts a weak sense of knowledge such as memorising rather educationally sterile facts or information with a strong sense of knowledge (or 'rich knowledge') with the notion of connected understanding of a human discipline area. It is interesting to note that Davis received rather robust criticism from Winch and Gingell (1996) who argued that so-called rich knowledge is difficult to assess and test for in reliable and valid ways and that the difference between weak and strong knowledge to some extent reflects the nuances of Platonic epistemology. Winch and Gingell (1996) do not deny that assessment is 'either *completely* reliable or valid' means of assessing learning, but quite rightly they argue that '*some* form of assessment is necessary if teaching is to take place' due to the important role assessment plays in teaching and learning, such as monitoring the success (or failure) of student learning (p. 380). My criticism is not a rehearsal of technical objections to the reliability or validity of assessment instruments, on the contrary, my complaint is a philosophical one to the effect that assessment, particularly large-scale public testing is incapable of assessing all forms of learning, or even the quality of student understanding because the instruments available are both too blunt and tend to capture a certain kind of knowledge that privileges theory over practice, and mental skills over physical skills. Take for instance the case offered by Carr (1984, 2003a) surrounding the difficulties of assessing dance knowledge. It is often misconceived under a shroud of empirical or behavioural conceptions of learning to simply involve checking whether the correct sequence of movements has been performed and mastered. Carr (2003a) argues that skill-acquisition is just one feature of learning to dance, but the dancer also needs to know about 'culturally nuanced *performance* knowledge', and so to properly assess dance would depend on the 'terpsichorical *performance* of *ritualised* actions' (p. 159). In this case, it is not that practical knowledge of dance can be assessed against certain public rules or principles; however, the persisting difficulty is that dance is an expressive and aesthetic art form of a unique kind that is difficult to quantify and qualify, and like other art forms is located in an area of constant contestability. Furthermore, the difference between subjective or expressive and logical or objective activities has more to do with the incommensurability between rival traditions of knowledge or rationality (see e.g. MacIntyre, 1981/2007, 1988, 1990, 1999; Stolz, 2015b). For the argument goes that artistic endeavours are inherently subjective due to their interpretative dimension, whereas mathematical propositions in the form of 2 + 3 = 5 have a certain objective certainty. Indeed, the effective teaching of the arts, such as dance and painting would necessarily require the initiation of students into the traditions of these practices which constitute specific knowledge, understanding and skills in order to bring about successful artistic expression. Although artistic and/or aesthetic knowledge may utilise qualitative judgements compared to the more formal logic of mathematics, there still exists a rational framework in which to judge these practices against certain internal standards of goods found within traditions to ascertain good (or bad) art (see e.g. MacIntyre, 1981/2007). Likewise, it is also worth reconsidering that not all subjects found within the school curriculum intentionally aim for the same logical order as mathematics. Indeed, Aristotle (2004, 1094b 25) would appear to reinforce this claim when he argues:

> … for it is the mark of the trained mind never to expect more precision in the treatment of any subject than the nature of the subject permits; for demanding logical demonstrations from a teacher of rhetoric is clearly about as reasonable as accepting mere plausibility from a mathematician.

The view that all subjects use or strive for the same formal deductive system of knowledge and understanding like mathematics, the sciences and so on is problematic because artistic and/or aesthetic knowledge are not based on precise axioms or principles. More importantly in this case, artistic and/or aesthetic knowledge cannot be as easily assessed against certain predetermined standards due to the nature of its activities. Indeed, the dance example highlights how practical knowledge should not be assessed in the same way as propositional or theoretical knowledge.[8] Likewise, it would also appear that certain activities such as dance, physical education and art are somehow resistant to summative assessment because they are not easily reducible to facts which can be tested for, or at least in the same way as say propositional or theoretical forms of knowledge found in mathematics, science and so on. Of course, it would be ill conceived to assume that certain forms of knowledge and understanding that are characteristic of distinct activities are resistant to educational assessment. If the central tenet of 'rich knowledge' is an understanding of how things 'connect' in a meaningful way, then it would be reasonable to conclude that this can occur in a diverse array of activities in the curriculum ranging from mathematics, to dance, to physical education, and so on. But the problem as I see it is to the effect that no matter how accurate assessment may become, particularly large-scale testing, in principle it can never assess all forms of learning or the quality of understanding because the instruments available are both too blunt and tend to capture a certain kind of knowledge that privileges theory over practice, and mental skills over physical skills. In saying this, I am certainly not arguing that all existing assessment instruments are inadequate to capture some student understanding of a certain kind—basic information and skills—but my issue is with the notion that assessment can measure all there may be or even the quality of understanding. As a result, the answer to my self-imposed question is intentionally cautious because some educational aims can easily be assessed (assuming that the tests are valid and reliable), such as low-level tests of numeracy and literacy; however, my argument has been that important aspects of education, such as student understanding and learning are not easily assessable in any substantive way. We should not lose sight of the fact that dance is not just about learning a sequence of movements, and mathematics is not just about the mechanical application of an arithmetical operation. Education is more complex than this, and any sense of understanding must involve the 'whys' and 'wherefores' of things. This means that large-scale public tests like NAPLAN are a very blunt assessment instrument that lends itself to 'teaching-to-the-test' because what can be tested are low-level skills and not student understanding and deep learning.

**Conclusion**

In this article, I have argued that assessment is a crucial part of any teaching endeavour, particularly as a mechanism to determine whether what has been taught has been learnt by students. I brought into question current trends in educational discourse which places a significant amount of emphasis upon large-scale public testing (NAPLAN) and reporting (My School website) that incorrectly infers a causal relationship between teaching and learning. Due to the conceptual confusion of this relationship, this has led many to fallaciously conclude that teachers should be held publicly accountable for raising educational standards. Central to this fallacious assumption is the manufacture of quality which uses assessment data in the form large-scale public tests such as NAPLAN as a mechanism of public accountability to its users (or purchasers). Understandably, this has exacerbated the 'teaching-to-the-test' syndrome and produced harmful effects using assessment as instruments of surveillance and control. It would appear that most of the objections surrounding assessment in education revolve around the nature of knowledge and how best to capture human knowledge and understanding. Although much philosophical disagreement still remains surrounding the role knowledge should play in education, I concluded that coming to know something is a *sine qua non* of any education. This then led to the self-imposed question: Can educationally significant learning be assessed?

In order to answer my self-imposed question, I caution that some educational aims can easily be assessed (assuming that the tests are valid and reliable), such as low-level tests of numeracy and literacy; however, my argument has been that important aspects of education, such as student understanding and learning are not easily assessable in any substantive way. To demonstrate what I meant, in the first section of my article, I briefly outlined how the Platonic view of knowledge has influenced educational epistemology to conclude that all forms of knowledge and understanding can be assessed. In turn, Plato's epistemology has been the catalyst for assessment that attempts to capture student learning of so-called objective knowledge which has led to the proliferation of large-scale public testing that attempts to measure and quantify in scientific terms student understanding and learning. In order to refute the claim that all student learning and understanding can be assessed, I introduced the example of dance to highlight that the assessment of dance is not the same as the assessment of mathematics. I make the point that dance is not just about learning a sequence of movements, and mathematics is not just about the mechanical application of an arithmetical operation. Education is more complex than this, and any sense of understanding must involve the 'whys' and 'wherefores' of things. Unfortunately, there has been no attempt by the government to do this under NAPLAN because such an assessment instrument is both too blunt an instrument to test for student understanding and deep learning, and tends to capture a certain kind of knowledge that privileges theory over practice, and mental skills over physical skills.

## Disclosure statement

No potential conflict of interest was reported by the author.

## Notes

1. See Plato's *Meno*, *Republic* and *Theaetetus* (see Hamilton & Cairns, 1961).
2. Other notable examples worth mentioning are The Organisation for Economic Co-operation and Development's Programme for International Student Assessment, the International Association for the Evaluation of Educational Achievement's Trends in International Mathematics and Science Study and Progress in International Reading Literacy Study and the Brooking Institution's Learning Metrics Task Force. For the point and purpose of this article, I will limit my discussion of large-scale public testing to NAPLAN as it relates to both my local context and what I know the most about.

3. The obvious question to ask here is Would teacher performance pay in schools exacerbate the 'teaching-to-the-test' syndrome? Currently this is a contentious issue in Victoria. At the time of writing the State Government of Victoria would like to introduce teacher performance pay in schools.
4. Tomazin (2013) reported in *The Sunday Age* more than 150 schools having been caught breaking rules surrounding the administration of NAPLAN. One disconcerting incident is worth noting of a teacher being reprimanded for providing answers to students during tests. This brings a new meaning to 'teaching-to-the-test'.
5. MacIntyre's unique brand of communitarianism broadly includes two elements: (1) individuals that belong to a community share *common* ends and (2) individuals that are members of the community derive their *sense of identity* from belonging to the group.
6. In the article titled 'Embodied learning', Stolz (2015a) provides an account of how humans come to understand meaningfully. The key concept outlined is that we 'come to' an understanding of something from our own point of view as a result of experiencing it. Since our engagement with the world is not just cognitive or theoretical, but involves the emotional, practical, aesthetic and so on because as beings-in-the-world, we are in open to the world we inhabit through the vehicle of one's own body.
7. Not only is this a narrow conception of education, it neglects the fact that a well-balanced education necessarily involves the development of the social, emotional, physical and so on.
8. For novel works on practical knowledge, see: 'The philosophy of G. Ryle and its significance for physical education: Some thoughts and reflections' (Stolz, 2013), and Chapter 3 from Stolz (2014).

## References

Aristotle. (2004). *Nicomachean ethics.* (Further revised ed., J. A. K. Thomson, Trans.). London: Penguin.

Carr, D. (1984). Dance education, skill, and behavioral objectives. *Journal of Aesthetic Education, 18,* 67–76.

Carr, D. (1992). Education, learning and understanding: The process and the product. *Journal of Philosophy of Education, 26,* 215–225.

Carr, D. (1994). Educational enquiry and professional knowledge: Towards a Copernican revolution. *Educational Studies, 20,* 33–52.

Carr, D. (1998). Towards a re-evaluation of the role of educational epistemology in the professional education of teachers. In S. Tozer (Ed.), *Philosophy of education* (pp. 439–447). Urbana, IL: Philosophy of Education Society.

Carr, D. (2000). Is teaching a skill? In R. Curren (Ed.), *Philosophy of education 1999* (pp. 204–212). Urbana, IL: Philosophy of Education Society.

Carr, D. (2001). Educational philosophy, theory and research: A psychiatric autobiography. *Journal of the Philosophy of Education, 35,* 461–476.

Carr, D. (2003a). *Making sense of education: An introduction to the philosophy and theory of education and teaching.* London: Routledge.

Carr, D. (2003b). Philosophy and the meaning of 'education'. *Theory and Research in Education, 1*, 195–212.
Carr, D. (2010). The goals of education. In J. Arthur & I. Davies (Eds.), *The Routledge education studies textbook* (pp. 9–18). London: Routledge.
Davis, A. (1995). Criterion-referenced assessment and the development of knowledge and understanding. *Journal of Philosophy of Education, 29*, 3–21.
Davis, A. (1996). Who's afraid of assessment? Remarks on Winch and Gingell's reply. *Journal of Philosophy of Education, 30*, 389–400.
Davis, A. (1999). *Educational assessment: A critique of educational policy, impact 1*. London: Philosophy of Education Society of Great Britain.
Gipps, C. (1994). *Beyond testing: Towards a theory of educational assessment*. London: The Falmer Press.
Hamilton, E., & Cairns, H. (Eds.). (1961). *Plato: The collected dialogues*. Princeton, NJ: Princeton University Press.
Hirst, P. H. (1965). Liberal education and the nature of knowledge. In R. D. Archambault (Ed.), *Philosophical analysis and education* (pp. 113–138). London: Routledge & Kegan Paul.
Hirst, P. H. (1971). What is teaching? *Journal of Curriculum Studies, 3*, 5–18.
Hirst, P. H. (1973). Liberal education and the nature of knowledge. In R. S. Peters (Ed.), *The philosophy of education* (pp. 87–111). Oxford: Oxford University Press.
Hirst, P. H. (1974). *Knowledge and the curriculum*. London: Routledge & Kegan Paul.
Jarvis, P. (2006). *The theory and practice of teaching* (2nd ed.). London: Routledge.
MacIntyre, A. (1981/2007). *After virtue* (3rd ed.). Notre Dame, IN: Notre Dame University Press. (First published in 1981).
MacIntyre, A. (1988). *Whose justice? Which rationality?* London: Duckworth.
MacIntyre, A. (1990). *Three rival versions of moral enquiry*. Notre Dame, IN: Notre Dame University Press.
MacIntyre, A. (1999). *Dependent rational animals: Why human beings need the virtues*. London: Duckworth.
Moore, A. (2004). *The good teacher*. London: Routledge.
Moore, A. (2012). *Teaching and learning: Pedagogy, curriculum and culture* (2nd ed.). London: Routledge.
Oakeshott, M. (1967). Learning and teaching. In R. S. Peters (Ed.), *The concept of education* (pp. 156–176). London: Routledge & Kegan Paul.
Peters, R. S. (1966). *Ethics and education*. London: Allen & Unwin.
Plato. (1961). Theaetetus. In E. Hamilton & H. Cairns (Eds.), *Plato: The collected dialogue* (pp. 845–919). Princeton, NJ: Princeton University Press.
Skinner, B. F. (1968). *The technology of teaching*. New York, NY: Appleton Century Crofts.
Stolz, S. A. (2013). The philosophy of G. Ryle and its significance for physical education: Some thoughts and reflections. *European Physical Education Review, 19*, 381–396.
Stolz, S. A. (2014). *The philosophy of physical education: A new perspective*. London: Routledge.
Stolz, S. A. (2015a). Embodied learning. *Educational Philosophy and Theory, 47*, 474–487.
Stolz, S. A. (2015b). MacIntyre, rival traditions and education. *Discourse: Studies in the Cultural Politics of Education*. Advance online publication. doi:10.1080/01596306.2015.1026880
Tomazin, F. (2013, February 17). Schools caught cheating on NAPLAN. *The Sunday Age*. Retrieved from http://www.theage.com.au/victoria/schools-caught-cheating-on-naplan-20130216-2ek6p.html
Winch, C. (1996a). Manufacturing educational quality. *Journal of the Philosophy of Education, 30*, 9–24.
Winch, C. (1996b). Satisfying the customer: Education in the marketplace. *Journal of Philosophy of Education, 30*, 97–112.
Winch, C., & Gingell, J. (1996). Educational assessment: Reply to Andrew Davis. *Journal of Philosophy of Education, 30*, 377–388.

# The Givenness of the Human Learning Experience and Its Incompatibility with Information Analytics

David Lundie

**Abstract**

*The rise of learning analytics, the application of complex metrics developed to exploit the proliferation of 'Big Data' in educational work, raises important moral questions about the nature of what is measurable in education. Teachers, schools and nations are increasingly held to account based on metrics, exacerbating the tendency for fine-grained measurement of learning experiences. In this article, the origins of learning analytics ontology are explored, drawing upon core ideas in the philosophy of computing, such as the general definition of information and the information-theoretic account of knowledge. Drawing upon a reading of Descartes Meditatio II, which extends the phenomenology of Jean-Luc Marion into a pedagogy of intentionality, the article identifies a fundamental incompatibility between the subjective experience of learning and the information-theoretic account of knowledge. Human subjects experience and value their own information incommensurably with the ways in which computers measure and quantify information. The consequences of this finding for the design of online learning environments, and the necessary limitations of learning analytics and measurement are explored.*

**Introduction**

The impact of learning analytics on contemporary education is pervasive, and has largely advanced without investigation of its informational ontology. Learning analytics denotes 'the measurement, collection, analysis and reporting of data about learners and their contexts, for purposes of understanding and optimising learning and the environment in which it occurs' (Siemens et al., 2011), but such a definition begs the question of what constitutes optimal learning. The range of data-sets used by learning analytics software to measure and optimise student learning includes highlighted text (SparTagUs), comprehension questions (Zementis-ADAPA) and visual models (Cognos), while approaches still in development measure at an even more minute level, using keystroke patterns and eye tracking to develop an increasingly granular model of the learning subject. Technologies currently under development effect a neurological reduction, promising real-time brain scanning in the classroom. While some of these applications may seem far into the future, there are few educators or educational administrators who are not familiar with a range of software packages promising predictivity based on baseline and continuing assessments. The availability of these fine-grained measures and their increasing importance has heralded fundamental shifts in the meaning of learning (Lundie, 2014a) which remain largely unexamined. Given the unforeseen impact which systems of assessment can have on learning (Nichol, 2012), and the bias which unreflective information systems design can introduce into their use (Friedman & Nissenbaum, 1996), an exploration of the epistemic assumptions underpinning learning analytics is both timely and pertinent.

I will argue that much of the present design processes and theories of learning analytics, by emphasising the mediation of learning, rather than the interaction which constitutes education, absent an important pedagogical dimension. The concepts of information and learning derived from information systems design are at best metaphors for human education, and fail to capture an important aspect of the *givenness* of human subjective experience. This *givenness* is explored here through a consideration of the Cartesian self.

The growth of learning analytics parallels that of the rise of 'Big Data', the proliferation of fine-grained metrics about all aspects of human life, gathered by an increasingly networked ambient environment. By some measures, more data is generated every two days than in the whole of human history up until 2003 (Siegler, 2010). Growing concerns over the growth and sharing of such multifaceted metrics, including the corporate acquisition of government data and government appropriation of corporate data by government, have led to calls for a digital charter to protect openness and individual freedom online (Lundie, 2014b).

For liberal conceptions of education, this granularity of measurement and control raises fundamental questions. As legal scholar Julie Cohen observes:

> Autonomous individuals do not spring full-blown from the womb. We must learn to process information and to draw our own conclusions about the world around us … 'Autonomy' constitutes an essential independence of critical faculty and an imperviousness to influence. But to the extent that information shapes behavior, autonomy is radically contingent upon environment and circumstance. The only tenable solution—if autonomy is not to degenerate into the simple stimulus-response behavior sought by direct marketers—is to underdetermine environment. (Cohen, 2000, p. 1400)

Besides the substantial moral questions raised by the prospect of increasing invasion into the learner's private thoughts (van den Hoven, 1997; Wolpe, Foster, &

Langleben, 2005), many learning analytics applications rely on an attenuated conception of learning, which has the potential to elide the most fundamentally human elements of education, at precisely the moment when human distinctiveness is most profoundly threatened by 'intelligent' systems of control (Floridi, 2005; Spencer, 1996). This article explores the epistemic foundations of information theory, central to the design of many 'intelligent' systems in the world of Big Data which includes learning analytics, and contrasts this with a phenomenology of human learning foundational to the European Enlightenment tradition from Descartes onwards, to illustrate a fundamental incompatibility.

In an insightful sociological analysis of the impact of digital analytics on education, Selwyn (2014) identifies six areas for further study in the ethical consideration of learning analytics:

1. What data exist in educational contexts?—including concern for the inter-operability and compatibility of data.
2. What are the 'primary' uses of these data?—in the case of learning analytics, the stated uses relate to optimisation, evaluative and formative assessment
3. What, if any, are the 'secondary' uses of these data?—relating to concerns of contextual integrity—data being shared and re-used in unintended contexts. (Solove, 1997)
4. What are the consequences of these uses of data?—relating to questions of informational injustice—accumulation of data being used to create a power differential between users and analysts. (Van den Hoven, 1997)
5. What organisational cultures have formed around the use of data within educational settings, and with what outcomes?—relating to emergent bias—the capacity of social uses of data systems to deflect from their stated purposes. (Friedman & Nissenbaum, 1996)
6. How might data work be more efficiently and equitably arranged in educational contexts?—again relating to the varieties of informational injustice. (Selwyn, 2014, pp. 13–14)

While ethical questions regarding the social uses of data have been extensively explored elsewhere, the analysis that follows is aimed at addressing the first and most fundamental of Selwyn's questions, whether the data of human learning are fundamentally compatible and inter-operable with information as conceptualised, gathered and processed in learning analytic systems as currently designed. It is not the intention of this paper to problematise all learning technologies (cf. Steigler, 2010), but rather to confine itself to a particular problem set—the reduction of human learning to that which is measurable and compatible with data gathered by analytics software. Whether learning, either as process or outcome, can be rendered inter-operable, with the call–response protocols by which machines exchange information, is an important and under-theorised question.

## The Information-Theoretic Conception

From its beginnings, information technology has engaged with philosophical questions in epistemology and ontology. Initially, the philosophy of information was largely concerned with the authentication of truth values in communication and machine manipulation of data. As such, it remained largely a sub-set of the philosophy of mathematics. Until recently, ethical discussions have been limited to the material effects of information technology, such as designing an air-traffic control system with fail-safes to prevent planes falling out of the sky in the event of communication failure. Under such a description, ethical systems are synonymous with efficient systems, and the social effects of their design or use are regarded as 'inherently value neutral' (Alder, 1998). More recently, however, increasing concerns have been raised about ethical issues inherent in information systems and their use (Loch & Conger, 1996), (Wicker & Schrader, 2010), recognising that the way information systems collect and present information can have profound effects on a range of social interactions from our understandings of privacy (Schrader, Yan, Lundie, & Schulze, 2011) to our employment opportunities (Spencer, 1996).

The information-theoretic account of knowledge, which has until recently been the dominant view in the philosophy of information and computing, attempts to address the problem of linking truth, knowledge and justification on the basis of information alone. Formally, this account states:

> K knows that s is F = K's belief that s is F is caused (or causally sustained) by the information that s is F. (Dretske, 1981)

This approach seeks to solve Gettier-type problems of justification which undermine positivist epistemology (Gettier, 1963) by positing only causal chains. All justifications are simply further information about information. This account requires a definition of information such that information is meaningful, well-formed data (Floridi, 2004). Such an account is highly satisfactory when designing systems for information transfer and authentication, and consequently occupies a prominent place in information technology. To define such transfer and authentication as constitutive of human learning, however, is potentially penurious, not least because the definition of information on which it rests: 'x is information that p if [and only if] p' (Dretske, 1981) requires recourse to some other, referentially grounded, epistemic consideration if the information world is not to float free of any referent in the 'real' world.

This mechanistic approach to knowledge is nothing new; in 1749, La Mettrie articulates an epistemology in many ways similar to the information-theoretic account of knowledge:

> sounds or words, which are transmitted from one person's mouth, through another's ear and into his brain. (de Mettrie, 1996, p. 13)

All sensory justifications, on this account, are information transmission. While Dretske does go on to nuance this theory, for instance by differentiating between 'structuring' causes which consist of information at the programming level and 'triggering' causes, when information acts upon that programme (Dretske, 1991,

p. 114), considering this to establish an explanatory connection between thought and action, and recognising that information does not equal meaning, he asserts that to explain 'why a system ... behaves the way it does, we are often asking a question that requires going outside the system for the answer' (Dretske, 1993, p. 209). Approaches to intelligence in information theory tend either towards an informational-causal monism or to posit the impossibility of the question due to the necessity of 'going outside' the system in order to answer the question of meaning. In drawing attention to a phenomenological model which recognises human conscious experience as neither caused nor dualistic or exterior to the material, I wish to challenge the inference inherent in the natural-language-use test for artificial intelligence. According to this test, a machine is intelligent if it is capable of using language in a way indistinguishable from an intelligent being (Turing, 2004). On such an account, there is no 'inside' to intelligence, no intelligent being, but merely an intelligence in the abstract, defined by its role in the causal chain. This causal reductivism has potentially penurious consssequences for education.

Contemporary attempts to situate machine learning in terms of symbol-grounding, enabling machines to associate information with referents in the world, still rely on this informational reduction of all data, and an equivalence between sense perception and information transmission, adding to it a further equivalence between subjective knowledge and sensory information. The symbol-grounding approach attempts to simulate in intelligent machinery a view of the brain which functions:

> by internalizing the process of creating m[eaningful]-representations. Rather than producing the representation in terms of external physical symbols (sounds, gestures ...) an internal image is created and re-entered and processed as if it was perceived externally. (Steels, 2008)

According to this view, the brain's internal 'imaging' can be understood as representational, in the same way as external sensory data. As such, the brain can be understood as an information processor, receiving information from its internal processing (memories and imagination) in the same way as other information channels. I will argue that this model is insufficient for the development of human learning because the causal account on which it rests is neither necessary nor sufficient to account for the phenomenon of human subjectivity, an essential prerequisite for learning.

In the absence of any non-informational justification, the information-theoretic conception of knowledge relies upon mathematical probability for epistemic certainty. The mathematical theory of communication proposes that information justifies knowledge in inverse proportion to probability (Shannon & Weaver, 1949). I have left my car door locked or unlocked, p = 'my car is unlocked' has two possible states, so one piece of information can determine the truth value of p. If I know that one car in the car park has been left unlocked, however, many more items of information may be required to determine p's truth value. Under this description, the more items of granular information can be gathered, the more certain an analytic system can be that learning outcomes have been met.

Furthermore, the General Definition of Information states that each item of information in this causal chain will be formed of *meaningful, well-formed* data (Floridi,

2004). This requires that the data can be understood, exchanged and interpreted in similar ways by more than one information processor.

I contend that this account of knowledge, while highly satisfactory for the design of information systems, is entirely unsuited to the nature of education because the epistemic value of learning is grounded in the learner as subject, not the data of learning content. As such, optimisation cannot be understood solely as a function of effective transmission of information through causal chains. Furthermore, the nature of human learning is grounded in a givenness which is irreducible to information transfer and incompatible with the general definition of information. Given that the success of information systems in use depends on the effective interaction between agents and mediating technologies (Ess, 2009), if the nature of one set of agents—the human learners—is fundamentally misunderstood in design, this can lead to bias in system use, with unforeseen social consequences (Friedman & Nissenbaum, 1996). In the case of Learning Analytics, the unforeseen consequences can be seen in the elision of value and intent from learning, and a focus on information transfer which reduces and trivialises learner autonomy. Furthermore, by relying on granular metrics to test the human learner's ability to complete a narrow set of tasks, involving the transfer and authentication of information (content knowledge and assessment), the stage is set for a form of education in which human learners are systemically subordinated to more efficient artificial information processors.

## The Learner as Intentional Subject

Some advocates of informational accounts of knowledge have drawn upon Cartesian conceptions of the logical self as a disembodied agent, separate from the world of objects about which information can be gathered, to ground an ontology of the human subject onto which information can be projected and processed (Bailey, 2005). This understanding of the knowing agent misrepresents or elides an essential element of the Cartesian project. As Jean-Luc Marion (2003) has argued, the Cartesian ego is not solipsistic or self-affirming, but exists through 'the originary interlocution of another who posits the *ego* in existence' (p. 49). In *Meditatio II*, Descartes posits:

> Nunquid est aliquis Deus, vel quocunque nomine illum vocem, qui mihi has ipsas cogitationes immitttit? [Is there not a God, or whatever he may be called, who gives me in myself the thoughts I am now having?] (Descartes, 2008)

From this, Marion infers the necessity of alterity to the Cartesian ego. Whether the ego is being persuaded or deceived, the structure of a dialogue posits a self. The ego's self-awareness on this account is not caused by a chain of information, which presupposes an information processor capable of giving meaning to the information. Instead, the ego encounters its *ipseity*, its selfhood, as given. This givenness enables the subject to know their existence but not to infer from this their essence. I may know that I am, but not know what it is that I am (Marion, 2003). Givenness is not equivalent to the 'ego cogito', the thought thinking about itself—'[t]hinking about [the thought] is one mode of givenness; it is another one altogether to find oneself in the presence of —what gives itself.' (Marion, 2002a, p. 29). In contrast to the informational-causal reduction on which much Learning Analytics research rests, this conception of the self, which presupposes a being, and a being-in-relation, in order to posit an intelligence, is essential to the pedagogical traditions which constitute both the liberal (cf. Morgan & Guilherme, 2010) and progressive (cf. Biesta, 2012) traditions in Western educational thought.

Marion's reading alludes to the Augustinian origins of the Cartesian project. In the Augustinian *anima*, the interior sense is distinguished from the causal chains of information which reach the subject from the senses or through interpersonal communication,

> of all which sensible objects it is the images resembling them [data], but not themselves, that we perceive in the mind and hold in the memory ... However, without any delusive representation of images or phantasms, I am most certain that I am, that I know, and that I delight in this ... for if I am deceived, I am. For he who does not exist cannot be deceived ... For, as I know that I am, so I know this also, that I know. And when I love these two [being and knowing], I add to them a third, that is, my love, which is of equal importance. (Augustine, City of God, XI, 26, 2007)

This tripartite structure of knowledge, being and love, in which Augustinian pedagogy finds an interior image of God 'for He who is said to reside in the interior man is Christ' (Augustine, De Magistro XI, 38, 1938) finds its parallel in the role of imagination as constitutive of the intentional ego-subject in Descartes' *Meditatio II*. In this regard, Marion's reading attempts to reintegrate ethics and epistemology (Marion, 2003) around the intentional. The good teacher is not only causally efficient, as the mechanical teacher may be, but is one who draws attention to the intentionality of being.

The canonical reading of Descartes is bound up with a separation between mind and world, subject and object. It is for this reason that information philosopher Luciano Floridi considers the Augustinian position towards the world to be dualistic (Floridi, 2008) and considers it fundamentally 'ontocentric', respectful of the natural order of the universe, 'a naturalistic philosophy that closely resonates with Spinoza, Plato, Confucius, and Buddhist thought (among others) in its affirmation of the intrinsic moral worth of the *cosmos* as such' (p. 193). Marion's highlighting of the fundamentally relational nature of the Cartesian ego, however, challenges such an account. In the second meditation, Descartes challenges the notion of personal identity as pertaining to the immaterial soul, responsible for such activity as 'me nutriri, incedere, sentire, et cogitare' (nourishment, motion, sense perception and thinking). Descartes is not introducing here an immateriality to personal being. Rather, he presumes it already on the basis of Christian and classical arguments, but then goes further to posit a grounding of the ego neither in body nor soul, but in a self-awareness which challenges, and imposes meaning upon, data concerning objects in the world.

Marion (2003) highlights that Descartes is unable to infer essence from existence; yet, having established that of all the attributes he ascribes to the soul, only thought establishes existence with certainty, Descartes immediately addresses to himself the question of essence:

> 'Quid praeterea? Imaginabor:' [What else am I? I will use my imagination] (Descartes, 2008, p. 36)

The purpose, then, of the ego, according to this reading is not a solipsistic refutation of the sceptics, but 'Nihil nisi punctum petebat Archimedes, quod esset firmum et immobile, ut integram terram loco dimoveret' (Descartes, 2008); not to separate itself from the world of objects, but to move or order the world. The imagination does precisely this, not by separating subject from object, but by orienting subject–object–telos. The role of imagination in the Cartesian ego bears clear parallels to that of love in the Augustinian soul. Love/imagination as animating principle attaches itself to the certainty of thought, and from it, of being. It is not only that the ego is aware of an informational item, which in the 2nd Meditation assumes an immediacy, no longer *cogito, ergo sum*, but *ego sum, ego existo* (Marion, 2003, p. 41), but this awareness implies agency. Having not previously thought about or known the nature of his being, nor had the author imagined (Descartes, 2008, p. 35) but having come to know, he comes also to imagine.

Only in considering the link between *ego, cogito and imaginatio* in the 2nd Meditation does a Cartesian pedagogy begin to suggest itself. In the analogy of the wax, Descartes sets up a fundamental element of human learning. While a causal chain of information is sufficient to knowing 'ipso sensu externo' the properties of the wax, it is only by 'potentia imaginatrice' (the power of imagination) that the author's perception, while it may be erroneous, 'non possum tamen sine humana mente percipere' (at least requires a human mind) (Descartes, 2008, p. 44). Drawing upon Augustine's third principle of the certainty of self-knowledge—love, the human mind, the mind of an intentional subject, is required for imaginative learning because only then is a project, a telos, and therefore a meaning, attached to free-floating data about the world. Without meaning, data does not become information.

The argument that an informational-causal chain is sufficient to account for knowledge thus fails in an important aspect of human subjectivity. This is so because, contrary to Steels' symbol-grounding conception of the brain, human subjects do not internalise the process of creating meaningful representations, (which is itself to beg the question of a further regress). Rather, the human subject is itself the locus of meaning.

The human mind is required for human learning, not to process knowledge, but to imagine, that is, to direct affection towards the act of coming to know. Beyond 'collective representations of the person there is a *unique* particularised singularity… the particular *isness* of the self' (Conroy, 2004, p. 6). This *isness* or intentionality, although enframed and situated in a network of cultural and technological interactions, nonetheless retains an irreducible interior complexity. It is not the alterity of the other which determines this inner realm, as though the data of self-knowledge were marked by meta-data which stated 'inner voice', while the data of interpersonal communication carry 'someone else's voice' meta-data. Rather, the recognition of incompleteness is a constitutive function of individual subjectivity (Conroy, 2009) and the subject is the locus and ground of meaning.

In attempting to account for this grounding of meaning in the subject, Marion describes responsibility in terms of gaze or witness. This is not a causal claim, akin to the downloading of a photograph, because the responsible agent's gaze necessarily entails affect. Augustine's *caritas*, Descartes' *imaginatio* and Marion's *responsibility* posit the immediacy of an irreducible human valuing of the phenomenon of knowing. Information is not necessary for the phenomenon because there is nothing 'behind' the phenomenon from which to form a causal chain, nor is information sufficient for the phenomenon, because data cannot account for this affective dimension to the gaze of the responsible subject. Marion posits three criteria for the givenness of the phenomenon, which by definition render it incompatible with an informational account of knowledge:

1. Intrinsic—givenness involves a bracketing out of the giver, there is no recourse to a cause
2. Irrevocable—the given is not reproducible or repeatable [it is in-dividual]
3. Radical—no gap exists between the givenness of a phenomenon and the phenomenon itself (Marion, 2002a, pp. 175–176)

The distinction here theorised is pre-ontological, making no claim about the materiality or otherwise of minds. Not only may it be grounded in divergent readings of Heideggerian phenomenology (Marion, 1998; Zahavi, 1999) but equally in divergent accounts of the Cartesian *cogito*, of which Heidegger was so famously critical. In contrast to the informational abstraction 'there is thought', as Levinas argues, Descartes' subject may be read as positing the intentional self as 'a thing that thinks' (Wyschogrod, 1990, p. 77). Far from merely 'the carrier of rational knowledge' (Bailey, 2005), the *isness* of this thinking thing has materiality and point of departure. Prior to executing any task, the subject as *cogito* in its relationship to materiality, temporality, in short to 'work', enters into a space of immediacy in the sense of not being a producer of inter-operable, mediatable information. It is not by detaching subject from object in service of metaphysical certainty (Bailey, 2005) that the working subject gives meaning to the world, but through the orientation of subject–object–end which constitutes meaningful work. This space is 'the most primordial object of utility' (Wyschogrod, 1990, p. 79) because by it a formative *experience* of the subject in contemplation of activity emerges, and it is from this intentional experience that any subsequent work proceeds. The thinking subject orders the world teleologically, with the thought itself among the objects of this ordering.

In contrast, for informational work, the outcome is always inherent in the programming, such that nothing is gained by its execution (Spencer, 1996), technological production assumes the self as planner, substituting a planned and datafied universe for the universe of givenness (Marion, 2002b). In learning which posits the learner as information processor, information passes through the subject, leaving the subject unchanged. Metrics predicated on call–response protocols encourage, or at least do not discourage, this form of work, the authentication-without-remainder of 'correct' informational transactions. It is not that the information present to the senses, mediated through a causal account of knowledge, is delusory as Descartes contended of the *camera obscura* (Descartes, 1954), but rather that information itself does not fulfil the causal relation between learning and acting in the human subject, which requires an act of intentionality.

Reducing givenness to the mathematical theory of communication, in which the quantity of information sufficient for knowledge is inversely proportional to probability, results in a paradox. On the canonical reading of Descartes, only the *ego cogito*, the thought, is required to establish self-knowledge. Given the phenomenon of thought, this single item of information is sufficient to verify p = 'I exist'. However, as the *ego*, the responsible subject, is itself the ground of meaning, and that meaning is given intrinsically, this datum is not meaningful or well formed according to the general definition of information. Consequently, this datum is not informational, and it follows that no information is required to verify p. This paradox is resolved with recourse to the intentional reading of *Meditatio II*: the givenness of the phenomenon is immediate, *ego cogito, ego existo*, so there is only one possible state of affairs, and no information is required to verify it. The quantity $Q$ of information required to assert p: the existence of the subject is at once $Q = 1$ and $Q = 0$, because given the phenomenon, the subject must exist. Because the subject remains always insufficient to its own informational truth-value, the subject is always incapable of fully appropriating itself, remaining 'strange from within' (Conroy, 2009, p. 147). The human call–response includes an intersubjectivity not found in computer information transfer protocols, the subject as gift is always other, the *ego* cannot 'authenticate itself without remainder' (Marion, 2002a, p. 290).

It is not, then, that self-knowledge and intentionality are immaterial, in the sense of the canonical dualist reading of Descartes, but rather that they are non-informational, being neither compatible with the general definition nor with a causal chain of knowledge. In contradistinction to the causal chain of authentication proposed by the information-theoretic account of knowledge, Marion draws attention to 'responsibility' as characteristic of the human call–response. Responsibility is not caused but given a function of:

> 'Mineness'—the characteristic according to which I am at issue, in person and without any possible substitution-... a claim imposes a choice on me; or better; that a claim poses *me* as the *there* where one might recognise oneself... In short, the claim does not destroy the irreducible identity-with-self by dismissing any *I* in me, but inversely, underscores and provokes it. (Marion, 1998, p. 201)

Inverting the symbol-grounding approach to interiority as the internalisation of symbols, the intentional or responsible subject requires that processes of symbolic self-representation or authorisation are to some extent metaphorical, any symbol being an imaginary representation of the irreducible self for the purposes of interaction. A causal chain of information is insufficient to account for the self-knowledge of the responsible subject, but it is also, importantly, unnecessary, because responsibility on this account consists in a response not reducible to authentication, and therefore to information.

In place of *Machine Man*, the account of the human subject set out above: given not caused; responsible not authenticated; intentional not informational is irreducible to an information-theoretic conception of knowledge. Human subjectivity is not reducible to repeatable, communicable or causally sustained data. Therefore, the data of human subjectivity cannot be regarded as meaningful or well formed according to the general definition of information. <u>Human learners as intentional subjects value their experience of learning incommensurably with information *simpliciter*.</u> In designing human–computer interaction for learning, this metaphorical leap between the irreducible intentional subject and the socio-technically constructed identity of the user must be borne in mind.

**Discussion and Conclusion**

Without the need to posit an immaterial ego-soul, as the canonical reading of Descartes would suggest, it is nonetheless possible to argue for something constitutive of human subjectivity which is both distinct from call–response chains of information and which manifests that distinction in materially significant ways, not merely as a reflective soul, but as a being acting in and giving meaning to the social and educational world. The intentional subject is the learner as lover of learning, imaginator and witness. Human subjects are distinguished from robots, databases and Turing machines, not by their response to any given problem set (Floridi, 2005) but because they value their own information incommensurably with information in the abstract, viewing it not as exchange value but as gift. My mother's maiden name has an exchange value as a password for my credit cards, but it has another value linked to memory, heritage and family. This latter value is intentional; it is mine not because ownership of it was transferred to me in a causal chain, rather its having value for me is inseparable from and coterminous with its being mine.

Learning analytics enables the collection, aggregation and multivariate analysis of large quantities of meta-data, information about information transactions, detailed data about how people come to know. This shifts the emphasis of pedagogical research from the interaction of learning subjects to the means by which those interactions are mediated. Meta-data is information according to the information-theoretic definition, it is meaningful when used to calculate the probability of a given state of affairs—how likely is it, given the number of words John reads in 60 s, that he will be capable of success in English Literature at AS Level. It is not information about the learner as subject—it is unconcerned with consciously willed dispositions or the intentions of the learner. Individuals generate meta-data without having any conscious sense of doing so—keystroke patterns, eye tracker movements, even brain states—this data can be aggregated to produce a complex and granular picture with remarkable predictive capacity, yet it entirely ignores conscious human subjectivity. As I hope to have demonstrated, the definitions of knowledge, learning and intelligence derived from the philosophy of computing, as commonly used in definitions of 'machine learning' or 'artificial intelligence', are at best metaphors for simulations of human-like processes. As metaphors, such terms are highly satisfactory in the design of systems. Design aimed at optimising human learning, however, requires first a recognition that these definitions are insufficient, and secondly an engagement with philosophical pedagogy and the human sciences. Failure to do so can result in a reductive call–response measure of optimal learning as the merest transmission of information. This reductive informationalism represents a clear and present threat to contemporary education.

The responsible human subject must respond '*for* the event as its witness... *to* the affection that his flesh undergoes in and through itself... *for* the scope of his own gaze' (Marion, 2002a, p. 293) and not merely to the call in a reductive call–response informational chain. This response is *for* learning, and not merely *to* content characterises intentionality, without which learning cannot be witting and willing, or authentically human.

Responding to the question of inter-operability and compatibility, the phenomenon of the human learning subject is not reducible to informational transactions. This conclusion need not be penurious for learning analytics, provided that the metaphorical character of 'learning' as measured by digital data is acknowledged in the design and use of systems. Attentive to the intentional and intersubjective character of human learning, data analytics can serve to optimise environments in which the imaginative and affective encounter is possible. The error of conflating such measures with the telos of human education must be avoided if education is not to be reduced to a series of fine-grained informational transactions. As measurement becomes ubiquitous in the social and educational world and machines gain exponentially in informational intelligence, it is essential that educators turn their attention towards making human learners more imaginative, responsible, cultivating attitudes of openness, gratitude and love towards knowledge. In so doing, it may indeed be possible to optimise the environment for that unique intentionality which characterises the education of persons.

## Disclosure statement

No potential conflict of interest was reported by the author.

## References

Alder, G. S. (1998). Ethical issues in electronic performance monitoring: A consideration of deontological and teleological perspectives. *Journal of Business Ethics, 17*, 729–743.
Augustine. (1938). *De Magistro*. London: Appleton.
Augustine. (2007). City of God, XI, 26. In G. Klima, F. Allhoff, & A. J. Vaidya (Eds.), *Medieval philosophy: Essential readings with commentary* (p. 117). Oxford: Blackwell.
Bailey, L. W. (2005). *The enchantments of technology*. Chicago: University of Illinois Press.

Biesta, G. (2012). The educational significance of the experience of resistance: Schooling and the dialogue between child and world. *Other Education, 1*, 92–103.

Cohen, J. (2000). Examined lives: Informational privacy and the subject as object. *Stanford Law Review, 52*, 1373–1438.

Conroy, J. C. (2004). *Betwixt and between: The liminal imagination, education and democracy*. New York, NY: Peter Lang.

Conroy, J. C. (2009). The enstranged self: Recovering some grounds for pluralism in education. *Journal of Moral Education, 38*, 145–164.

de Mettrie, J. O. (1996). *Machine man and other writings*. Cambridge: Cambridge University Press.

Descartes, R. (1954). La Dioptrique [The formation of lenses]. In E. Anscombe & P. Geach (Eds.), *Descartes' philosophical writings* (pp. 241–256). Indianapolis, IN: Bobbs-Merrill.

Descartes, R. (2008). *Meditations on first philosophy: With selections from the objections and replies*. Oxford: Oxford University Press.

Dretske, F. (1991). How beliefs explain: Reply to Baker. *Philosophical Studies, 63*, 113–117.

Dretske, F. (1993). Can intelligence be artificial? *Philosophical Studies, 71*, 201–216.

Dretske, F. I. (1981). *Knowledge and the flow of information*. Cambridge, MA: MIT Press.

Ess, C. (2009). Floridi's philosophy of information and information ethics: Current perspectives, future directions. *The Information Society, 25*, 159–168.

Floridi, L. (2004). Information. In L. Floridi (Ed.), *The Blackwell guide to the philosophy of computing and information* (pp. 40–62). Oxford: Blackwell.

Floridi, L. (2005). Consciousness, agents and the knowledge game. *Minds and Machines, 15*, 415–444.

Floridi, L. (2008). Information ethics: A reappraisal. *Ethics and Information Technology, 10*, 189–204.

Friedman, B., & Nissenbaum, H. (1996). Bias in computer systems. *ACM Transactions on Information Systems, 14*, 330–347.

Gettier, E. (1963). Is justified true belief knowledge? *Analysis, 23*, 121–123.

Loch, K. D., & Conger, S. (1996). Evaluating ethical decision making and computer use. *Communications of the ACM, 39*, 74–83.

Lundie, D. (2014a). Educational technology, the philosophy of information and the education of the human. In D. Lewin & M. White (Eds.), *New directions in the philosophy of education* (pp. 45–58). London: Bloomsbury Academic.

Lundie, D. (2014b). Theorising relational privacy: Embodied perspectives to support ethical professional pedagogies. In D. Bridges & P. Smeyers (Eds.), *Springer international handbook of interpretation in education* (pp. 1481–1498). London: Springer.

Marion, J.-L. (1998). *Reduction and givenness: Investigations of Husserl, Heidegger and phenomenology*. Evanston, IL: Northwestern University Press.

Marion, J.-L. (2002a). *Being given: Toward a phenomenology of givenness*. Stanford, CA: Stanford University Press.

Marion, J.-L. (2002b). *Prolegomena to charity*. New York, NY: Fordham University Press.

Marion, J.-L. (2003). The original otherness of the ego: A rereading of Descartes Meditatio II. In E. Wyschgood & G. P. McKenny (Eds.), *The ethical* (pp. 33–53). Oxford: Blackwell.

Morgan, W. J., & Guilherme, A. (2010). *I and Thou:* The educational lessons of Martin Buber's dialogue with the conflicts of his times. *Educational Philosophy and Theory, 44*, 979–996.

Nichol, D. (2012). Resituating feedback from the reactive to the proactive. In D. Boud & L. Malloy (Eds.), *Effective feedback in higher and professional education: Understanding it and doing it well* (p. 34). London: Routledge.

Schrader, D. E., Yan, J., Lundie, D., & Schulze, W. (2011). *How much do people value privacy?* Tucson, AZ: North American Economic Science Association Conference.

Selwyn, N. (2014). Data entry: Towards the critical study of digital data and education. *Learning, Media and Technology*. Ahead of Print. doi:10.1080/17439884.2014.921628

Siegler, M. G. (2010, August 4). *TechCrunch: Eric Schmidt: Every 2 days we create as much information as we did up to 2003.* Retrieved May 5, 2014, from http://techcrunch.com/2010/08/04/schmidt-data/

Siemens, G., Gasevic, D., Haythornthwaite, C., Dawson, S., Shum, S., Ferguson, R., ... Baker, R. (2011). Open learning analytics: An integrated and modularized platform. *Society for Learning Analytics Research.* Retrieved from http://www.solaresearch.org/OpenLearningAnalytics.pdf

Shannon, C. E., & Weaver, W. (1949). *The mathematical theory of communication.* Urbana: University of Illinois Press.

Solove, D. (1997). *The digital person: Technology and privacy in the information age.* New York: NYU Press.

Spencer, G. (1996). Microcybernetics as the meta-technology of pure control. In Z. Sardar & J. R. Ravetz (Eds.), *Cyberfutures: Culture and politics on the information superhighway* (pp. 61–76). London: Pluto Press.

Steels, L. (2008). *The symbol grounding problem has been solved, so what's next? Symbols, embodiment and meaning.* New Haven, CT: Academic Press.

Steigler, B. (2010). *Taking care of youth and the generations.* Stanford, CA: Stanford University Press.

Turing, A. (2004). Intelligent Machinery. In B. J. Copeland (Ed.), *The Essential Turing* (pp. 395–409). Oxford: Clarendon.

van den Hoven, M. J. (1997). Privacy and the varieties of moral wrong-doing in an information age. *ACM SIGCAS Computers and Society, 27,* 33–37.

Wicker, S., & Schrader, D. (2010). Privacy-aware design principles for information networks. *Proceedings of the IEEE, 99,* 330–350.

Wolpe, P. R., Foster, K. R., & Langleben, D. D. (2005). Emerging neurotechnologies for lie-detection: Promises and perils. *The American Journal of Bioethics, 5,* 39–49.

Wyschogrod, E. (1990). *Saints and postmodernism: Revisioning moral philosophy.* Chicago, IL: University of Chicago Press.

Zahavi, D. (1999). *Self-awareness and alterity: A phenomenological investigation.* Evanston, IL: Northwestern University Press.

# A Quantum Measurement Paradigm for Educational Predicates: Implications for validity in educational measurement

Ian Cantley

**Abstract**

*The outcomes of educational assessments undoubtedly have real implications for students, teachers, schools and education in the widest sense. Assessment results are, for example, used to award qualifications that determine future educational or vocational pathways of students. The results obtained by students in assessments are also used to gauge individual teacher quality, to hold schools to account for the standards achieved by their students, and to compare international education systems. Given the current high-stakes nature of educational assessment, it is imperative that the measurement practices involved have stable philosophical foundations. However, this article casts doubt on the theoretical underpinnings of contemporary educational measurement models. Aspects of Wittgenstein's later philosophy and Bohr's philosophy of quantum theory are used to argue that a quantum theoretical rather than a Newtonian model is appropriate for educational measurement, and the associated implications for the concept of validity are elucidated. Whilst it is acknowledged that the transition to a quantum theoretical framework would not lead to the demise of educational assessment, it is argued that, where practical, current high-stakes assessments should be reformed to become as 'low-stakes' as possible. This article also undermines some of the pro high-stakes testing rhetoric that has a tendency to afflict education.*

**Introduction**

This article challenges the theoretical foundations of contemporary educational measurement models and proposes an alternative paradigm for the measurement of educational predicates. It is argued that current educational measurement practices are based upon a Newtonian conception of measurement. The quantum pioneer Niels Bohr was adamant, however, that the properties of intentional psychological predicates (such as learning) fit the framework of quantum theory, which superseded

Newtonian mechanics (that functions perfectly well for macrosystems) as the best physical model of microsystems in the early part of the twentieth century. Although Bohr referred to structural parallels between quantum theory and psychology (and, by extension, education), he never developed these claims; they are, however, investigated in this article. Ludwig Wittgenstein's later philosophy contains an extensive analysis of the nature of intentional predicates, and this is used, together with Bohr's philosophy of quantum mechanics, to demonstrate that a quantum theoretical paradigm would, in fact, provide a more secure basis for educational measurement. Finally, the implications of a transition from a Newtonian to a quantum theoretical framework for the concept of validity in educational measurement are considered.

**Psychology's 'Physics Envy'**

From the advent of psychology, some psychologists have sought to have the discipline recognized as a quantitative science and, according to Lagemann (2000), educational researchers simply followed suit. In formulating quantitative theories, psychologists re-defined measurement to suit their own purposes and attempted to measure psychological attributes, such as cognitive abilities, in the same way as the properties of macroscopic bodies are measured in Newtonian physics (Bruner, 1990). For example, item response theory is used in conjunction with structural equation modelling to estimate ability levels of individuals from their responses to test items. In this approach, it is assumed that ability levels can be abstracted away from the measuring instrument in the same way as a measurement of a dynamic attribute of a macroscopic body in Newtonian mechanics.

Michell (1997) casts considerable doubt on the legitimacy of contemporary approaches to psychological measurement. He asserts that, for measurements of psychological attributes to be legitimate, what he refers to as the 'scientific task' (Michell, 1997, p. 359) of measurement must be properly investigated prior to commencing work on the 'instrumental task' (Michell, 1997, p. 359). In other words, it is vital to demonstrate that psychological attributes are quantitative, and therefore measurable, before devising methods for actually measuring them.

Michell (1997, 1999) argues that, since psychological attributes lack additivity, they cannot be continuous quantities of the type encountered in Newtonian physics. According to Michell (1999, p. 71), additivity of an attribute is demonstrated if there is an actual physical process for combining magnitudes of the attribute so that:

(1) $w + x = x + w$ for any two magnitudes, $w$ and $x$, of the attribute, and
(2) $(w + x) + y = w + (x + y)$ for any three magnitudes $w$, $x$ and $y$ of the attribute, and
(3) The combined magnitude of the attribute is unchanged if equivalent objects are substituted—objects which have the same magnitudes as the individual objects that are being combined.

For example, combining two objects on a single set of weighing scales would be such a method in the case of weight. Michell's thesis is that there is no such process for combining magnitudes of psychological attributes such as cognitive abilities. As a consequence of his extensive critique of psychological measurement, in which he appeals to the mathematical foundations of measurement, Michell concludes as follows: 'These observations confirm that psychology, as a discipline, has its own definition of measurement, a definition quite unlike the traditional concept used in the physical sciences' (Michell, 1997, p. 360). Boring (1929) points out that the pioneers of psychology quickly came to realize that if psychology was not a quantitative discipline which facilitated measurement, psychologists could not adopt the epithet 'scientist' for 'there would ... have been little of the breath of science in the experimental body, for we hardly recognise a subject as scientific if measurement is not one of its tools' (Michell, 1990, p. 7).

The general definition of measurement accepted by most quantitative psychologists and educationalists is that formulated by Stevens (1946), which states: 'measurement is the assignment of numerals to objects or events according to rule' (Michell, 1997, p. 360). Stevens realized that, by predicating measurement just upon numerical representation, without the need for additivity, he could ratify and legitimize the measurement practices used by psychologists and liberate them from the need to test the underlying quantitative structure of psychological attributes. One of the consequences of this is that psychologists/educationalists assign numbers to attributes according to some pre-determined rule and do not consider the need to justify the measurement procedures used so long as the rule is followed. For example, psychologists/educationalists use total test scores to measure cognitive abilities without considering the need to justify their rationale for doing so. Stevens' rather vague definition distances measurement practices in psychology and education from measurement in classical Newtonian physics.

A fundamental notion in quantum theory is that a measured attribute can only be understood in the context of the measurement situation. This facet of the quantum realm is in stark contrast to the Newtonian worldview. In Newtonian physics, systems possess their attributes intrinsically and measurement is construed as a process for checking up on some pre-existing property of the system. Niels Bohr, who is widely regarded as the father of quantum theory, identified 'unambiguous communication', rather than quantification, as the hallmark of science. To communicate measurement results unambiguously in quantum theory, it is essential to factor in a description of the measuring instrument: the entity to be measured and the measuring instrument are non-separable.

The transition in physics from a Newtonian to a quantum theoretical model of reality should have had implications for psychology (Gigerenzer, 1987) and therefore also for education. Bruner (1990, p. xiii) warns that:

> The study of the human mind is so difficult, so caught in the dilemma of being both the object and the agent of its own study, that it cannot limit its enquiries to ways of thinking that grew out of yesterday's physics.

Bruner is referring to the difficulty of dividing up the mind into that which is the object of introspection (some region of the mind) and the introspecting agent (the mind itself). Bohr also refers to exactly the same problem:

> The epistemological problem under discussion may be characterized briefly as follows: For describing our mental activity, we require, on one hand, an objectively given content to be placed in opposition to a perceiving subject, while, on the other hand, as is already implied in such an assertion, no sharp separation between object and subject can be maintained, since the perceiving subject also belongs to our mental content. (Bohr, 1934/1987, p. 96)

Bohr believed that psychology and quantum theory share a common goal: to use ordinary language, learned through direct experience, to describe what transcends direct experience. He was of the view that he had identified an 'epistemological argument common to both fields' (Bohr, 1958/1987, p. 27). Similar claims have been made by other quantum pioneers, for example: 'It is the occurrence of similar concepts and thought models in both physics and psychology that makes Pauli so certain that they rest on a foundation of shared structures' (Gieser, 2005, p. 345).

The author draws on aspects of Wittgenstein's later philosophy and Bohr's philosophy of quantum mechanics to argue that education and psychology share the same 'measurement problem' as Bohr's so-called Copenhagen interpretation of quantum theory. Wittgenstein's philosophy of psychology is utilized since the eminent quantum physicist Werner Heisenberg links the Copenhagen interpretation to Wittgenstein's later philosophy (Stapp, 1972, p. 1114). Wittgenstein's later philosophical writings are used to establish that it is meaningless to ascribe a definite ability to an unmeasured individual; the ascription of a definite ability is only meaningful in a specific measurement context. In particular, if learning is construed as following simple rules to 'go beyond the information given' (Bruner, 1996, p. 129), it is evident that Wittgenstein's extensive analysis of rule following has implications for educational measurement. Accordingly, the following section summarizes this important aspect of Wittgenstein's later philosophy. The process of going beyond given information can be illustrated most effectively using mathematical rule following, but the ideas apply to all rule following from speaking a language to playing chess.

**Wittgenstein's Analysis of Rule Following**

Wittgenstein (Wittgenstein, 2009, §185) considers a scenario in which a child continues the arithmetical sequence 0, 2, 4, 6, ... beyond 1000 by writing 1000, 1004, 1008, 1012 and so on. Wittgenstein argues that there is a possibility the child has understood the order to continue the sequence as the community of mathematicians would understand the instruction 'Add 2 up to 1000, 4 up to 2000, 6 up to 3000 and so on'. Wittgenstein is using this example to communicate that, on the basis of a finite number of illustrations of a rule (the rule for the sequence of even numbers in this case), it is possible to attach multiple interpretations to the rule.

In the latter part of the twentieth century, cognitivism superseded behaviourism as the dominant psychological paradigm for understanding mental functions. It therefore seems uncontroversial to view the source of the child's ability to follow a rule as a finite object in his or her mind, and an obvious contender for this in the case of mathematical rule following is a formula. However, having a formula in mind is insufficient to explain mathematical rule following behaviour since, in Wittgenstein's view, a rule by itself leads to a paradox in that, on the basis of some interpretation of its requirements, any answer can be made to accord or to conflict with the rule:

> This was our paradox: no course of action could be determined by a rule, because every course of action can be brought into accord with the rule. The answer was: if every course of action can be brought into accord with the rule, then it can also be brought into conflict with it. And so there would be neither accord nor conflict here. (Wittgenstein, 2009, §201)

For example, it is possible for a child to write 10 (as one would expect) or −230 (as one would not expect) when he or she is asked to supply the next term in the sequence 2, 4, 6, 8, ... . The child who gives 10 as their answer is attaching the orthodox interpretation $u_n = 2n$, while the child who proffers −230 can claim to be acting in accord with the instruction to continue the sequence by attaching the interpretation $u_n = 2n - 10\ (n-1)\ (n-2)\ (n-3)\ (n-4)$ since both formulae clearly yield the given first four terms of the sequence.

It is over-simplistic to posit that, if God were to search the contents of the child's mind and uncover the formula $u_n = 2n$, then the child *must* supply 10 as the next term in the sequence 2, 4, 6, 8, ... . Analogously, discovery of the formula $u_n = 2n - 10\ (n-1)\ (n-2)\ (n-3)\ (n-4)$ does not guarantee that the child will proffer −230 as the fifth even number. The child may indeed have the formula $u_n = 2n$ in mind but be unable to use it correctly. Merely having a mental object (the formula in this case) before one's mind may be insufficient since the child may be unable to interpret the object correctly. Perhaps the characteristic which distinguishes the child, who can successfully go on to apply a formula correctly from the child who cannot, is the possession of a further mental object which permits the child to attach the correct interpretation to the formula. Unfortunately, this will not resolve the conundrum since, if the mind is construed as being populated by mental objects (formulae, images and so on) which require interpretation, an infinite regress ensues as follows:

> If it [the rule] requires interpretation, that could be done in lots of ways. So how do I tell which interpretation is correct? Does that, for instance, call for a *further* rule—a rule for determining correct interpretation of the original—and if so, why does it not raise the same difficulty again, thereby generating a regress? (Wright, 2001, p. 163)

It is thus evident that an appeal to interpretations does not settle whether the child should offer 10 or −230 as the fifth even number. Having a formula before one's mind does not guarantee the subsequent correct use of that formula and the introduction of interpretation cannot resolve the problem.

Wittgenstein (2009) anticipates that there may be an attempt to rescue the situation by introducing the idea of a Platonic mechanism in the child's mind, which gives the child access to all potential future applications of a rule without the need for interpretation or, indeed, any act of creativity on the child's part. In this situation, the child would be following a 'rules-as-rails' model where the rules 'somehow reach ahead of us and determine of themselves every actual and counterfactual proper application' (Wright, 2001, p. 163). Wittgenstein, however, rejected such an explanation of rule following, as illustrated by his view of mathematical rule following: 'The mathematician is an inventor, not a discoverer' (Wittgenstein, 1978, I, §168).

In Wittgenstein's view, private rule following within the realm of one's mind is impossible since the public criteria associated with a well-established practice (into which the rule-follower must be enculturated through training) are used to judge correct and incorrect applications of a rule:

> '[F]ollowing a rule' is a practice. And to *think* one is following a rule is not to follow a rule. And that's why it's not possible to follow a rule 'privately'; otherwise, thinking one was following a rule would be the same thing as following it. (Wittgenstein, 2009, §202)

Wittgenstein's appeal to public, behavioural criteria in his exegesis of rule following, rather than focusing on associated inner mental states and processes might be construed as indicating that his views are aligned with behaviourism. Wittgenstein, however, denies that he endorses behaviourism when he says 'If I speak of a fiction, then it is of a *grammatical* fiction' (Wittgenstein, 2009, §307) in response to the following questions posed by the interlocutor: 'Aren't you ... a behaviourist in disguise? Aren't you nevertheless basically saying that everything except human behaviour is a fiction?' (Wittgenstein, 2009, §307). Contrary to some readings of Wittgenstein, he does not deny the existence of mental states and processes. Rather, he posits that mental states are inextricably linked to outer behaviour: 'An "inner process" stands in need of outward criteria' (Wittgenstein, 2009, §580). Wittgenstein denies that mental states stand in a direct causal relation to outer behaviour, as per a Newtonian paradigm. Interestingly, he actually steers a path between cognitivism and behaviourism when he asserts, in relation to the nature of mental states, 'It's [a mental state] not a Something, but not a Nothing either! The conclusion was only that a Nothing would render the same service as a Something about which nothing can be said' (Wittgenstein, 2009, §304). In this quotation, Wittgenstein is rejecting the notion that, in following a rule for example, an individual is guided by some type of mental object (a 'something') which is hidden behind behaviour or indeed that rule following is reducible without residue to outer behaviour, so that what remains within is a 'nothing'.

The following section sets out the rationale for adopting a quantum theoretical measurement paradigm in education. In addition, Wittgenstein's later philosophy, and his analysis of rule following in particular, is used to establish a set of equivalences between the study of educational/psychological predicates and the study of quantum predicates.

**The Study of Educational Predicates: Quantum Analogues**

Why should a theory formulated for analysing the behaviour of microentities such as electrons apply to the study of psychological predicates of interest to educationalists such as learning, thinking, understanding and so on? According to Bohr, the primary concern of the quantum physicist is to communicate unambiguously about aspects of reality which are not visible to the human eye, using ordinary language developed to make sense of the world of everyday experience. The constructs of interest to quantum theorists, such as electrons and photons, manifest themselves in macroscopic measuring devices which can be read by the human eye. Physicists then communicate their experimental findings to colleagues using ordinary language supplemented by some specialist vocabulary.

The predicates of interest to psychologists and educationalists similarly cannot be observed directly but, rather, manifest themselves in the responses of individuals to measuring instruments such as tests. The words 'position' and 'velocity' function perfectly well when used to characterize the motion of tennis balls, for example, but cannot be used in common-sense ways to describe electrons and photons, which cannot be observed directly. Bohr, however, insists that everyday concepts like position and velocity must be retained in quantum theory but used in a more restrictive way, in the sense that it is necessary to factor in a description of the measuring instrument when referring to a measurement of position or velocity in the quantum realm. It is argued in this article that similar restrictions need to be placed on measurements of abilities in education, i.e. it is necessary to refer to the ability of an individual with respect to a particular question on a test rather than referring to ability as an attribute that exists independently of an act of measurement.

*The Analogue of Quantization*

In quantum theory, quantized attributes can only take certain discrete values. For example, the polarization of a photon is a quantized attribute since, for each direction, there are only two possibilities: either the photon is completely polarized in that direction or it is completely polarized perpendicular to that direction.

Wittgenstein rejects the notion that a psychological attribute, such as understanding or ability, is purely a mental process: 'In the sense in which there are processes (including mental processes) which are characteristic of understanding, understanding is not a mental process' (Wittgenstein, 2009, §154). This implies that, when one attempts to measure a psychological attribute such as ability, the measurement process cannot simply be a mechanism for checking up on the attribute. Consequently, it is meaningless to posit that a general ability, of the type a test purports to measure, can be measured in the Newtonian sense. Consider an $n$-item mathematics test consisting of questions $Q_1, Q_2, Q_3, ..., Q_n$, where the response to each question is either correct or incorrect. In Wittgenstein's view, 'it's not possible to follow a rule "privately"' (Wittgenstein, 2009, §202), and thus, ability *with respect to a given question* must be publicly demonstrated. Wittgenstein advocates the need for an individual to repeatedly demonstrate conformity with a rule-governed practice (such as addition) before one can ascribe the ability to use the rule correctly to the individual. In reality, however, high-stakes educational assessments do not usually test the application of a particular rule on multiple occasions, and it is thus necessary to refer to the ability to apply a rule *in the context of a particular question*, which represents a deviation from Wittgenstein's conception of demonstrating ability.

Furthermore, an individual will not have their ability with respect to a given question 'in their mind' either before or after they answer the question and, therefore, their ability with respect to the question will be indeterminate both before and after they respond to it. It is noteworthy that the degree of uncertainty pertaining to the ability with respect to a particular question will be greater before the question is attempted than afterwards. The individual's ability with respect to a given question will, however, be maximally certain at the instant they answer it, and this reinforces the fact that it is necessary to refer to their ability *with respect to a particular question*. Therefore, an individual's ability is a relational attribute in the sense that it can only be spoken of in conjunction with a specific question on the test. In conformity with quantum theory, a measurement of ability and the measuring device, i.e. the mathematical practice that is being tested by the question, form an indivisible whole and it is meaningless to refer to the measurement without referring to the measuring device. The need to refer to the ability of an individual with respect to a particular question undermines the rationale for calculating total test scores (which are often purported to represent ability in a particular area), since the summing of item scores on a test is predicated on the notion that each item is measuring the same construct, e.g. 'mathematical ability'. It is meaningless to combine scores in this way because no single ability exists.

At the instant, when a pupil answers a particular question, $Q_r$, their ability with respect to $Q_r$ (the measuring instrument) will be known. In other words, the pupil will have responded either correctly to $Q_r$ (i.e. in conformity with the criteria associated with the relevant practice that is being assessed by $Q_r$), thus affirming their ability with respect to $Q_r$, or incorrectly. Since there are only two discrete possibilities for each question, correct or incorrect, the pupil's ability with respect to each test item is a quantized attribute.

*The Analogue of Heisenberg's Uncertainty Principle*

Heisenberg's uncertainty principle, which is an important tenet of quantum theory, states that it is impossible to measure precisely both the position and the momentum of a microentity simultaneously.

Consider again an *n*-item mathematics test consisting of questions $Q_1$, $Q_2$, $Q_3$, ..., $Q_n$, where the response to each question is either correct or incorrect. If an individual responds to question $Q_r$ at time $t_r$, their ability with respect to $Q_r$ will be maximally certain at time $t_r$. Again, since Wittgenstein posits that a rule cannot be followed privately (Wittgenstein, 2009, §202), the individual's ability with respect to $Q_r$ will be unknown either before or after $t_r$. Similarly, if the individual answers question $Q_s$ at time $t_s$ (where $s \neq r$), their ability with respect to $Q_s$ will be maximally certain at time $t_s$ but unknown either before or after $t_s$. Clearly, it is impossible for the individual to respond to two questions simultaneously and, therefore, it is only possible for the ability of the individual to be known with respect to a single question at any instant in time. This is the analogue of Heisenberg's uncertainty principle in quantum theory.

*The Analogue of Wave Function Collapse*

In quantum theory, a microentity does not possess its dynamic attributes before a measurement is made. Rather, the microentity exists in a superposition of different states, which correspond to the possible outcomes of the measurement process. A dynamic attribute of the microentity only manifests itself at the point of measurement when the microentity interacts with a measuring device. This interaction gives rise to a sudden and discontinuous jump in the relevant dynamic attribute of the microentity from a superposition of all possible values, with associated probabilities, to one actual measurement result. The probability wave function, which incorporates information on all of the possible values and their respective probabilities, collapses to yield a single value at the point of measurement.

Wittgenstein offers support for the applicability of the notion of wave function collapse to the study of psychological and educational predicates when he argues that there is always a 'jump' to make between a concept and its application in a particular context:

> In all language there is a bridge between the sign and its application. No one can make this for us; we have to bridge the gap ourselves. No explanation ever saves the jump, because any further explanation will itself need a jump. (Wittgenstein, 1982, p. 67)

Consider once again an $n$-item mathematics test consisting of questions $Q_1$, $Q_2$, $Q_3$, ..., $Q_n$, where the response to each question is either correct or incorrect. Suppose also that the probability of an individual answering the question $Q_r$ correctly is $p_r$. Immediately before an individual answers $Q_r$, their ability with respect to $Q_r$ will, according to Wittgenstein's paradox of interpretation (discussed in the section on rule following), be characterized by a superposition of two different states corresponding to the two possible outcomes of their response to $Q_r$:

(1) correct response to $Q_r$, with associated probability $p_r$, and
(2) incorrect response to $Q_r$, with associated probability $1 - p_r$.

According to Wittgenstein (2009), the pupil in isolation could, under some interpretation of the requirements of $Q_r$, construe either the correct or an incorrect answer to $Q_r$ as correct. For example, Kripke (1982) considers a situation in which an individual who has only previously added whole numbers less than 57 asserts that the correct answer to the mathematical question 'What is 68 + 57?' is '5' rather than '125'. Kripke (1982) argues that it is possible the individual is using an alternative interpretation of '+' whereby the '+' symbol is being used to denote what he calls the 'quus' function instead of ordinary arithmetic addition. Kripke (1982) defines the rule for the 'quus' function, which he denotes by '⊕', as follows:

$x \oplus y = x + y$ if $x, y < 57$
$x \oplus y = 5$ otherwise.

Prior to the individual answering the question, they are in a superposition of two states (their answer is both '125' *and* '5'), but when they actually answer the question, the superposition collapses to just one answer (either '125' *or* '5').

Prior to actually answering $Q_r$, the individual's ability with respect to $Q_r$ is in a superposition of two states simultaneously. However, at the instant when the individual answers $Q_r$, the superposition of the two states 'correct' and 'incorrect' will collapse to just one: the actual measurement of the pupil's ability with respect to $Q_r$.

The assessor's knowledge of the pupil's ability with respect to $Q_r$ jumps instantaneously from an uncertain state to a certain state, since the pupil's actual answer to $Q_r$ will be either correct or incorrect. The process of measurement results in a sudden jump in the assessor's knowledge of the pupil's ability with respect to $Q_r$, from a combination of possible outcomes, each with an associated probability, to one actual outcome. The assessor's knowledge of the relevant ability changes from indeterminate to determinate. The sudden jump in the assessor's knowledge of the pupil's ability with respect to $Q_r$ is the analogue of the process of wave function collapse in quantum theory.

*The Analogue of Complementarity*

Bohr's principle of complementarity is a central feature of the Copenhagen interpretation of quantum theory. In the quantum world, some observations can never be made simultaneously. For example, one cannot observe a microentity as both a particle and as a wave at the same time. A microentity behaves as a particle when it is observed, but is characterized by a probability wave between observations. The two situations cannot occur simultaneously, i.e. they are mutually exclusive, but both are necessary to fully describe the microentity's nature. Bohr believed that the complementarity principle accommodates the paradoxical nature of the wave-particle duality exhibited by microentities. He contended that 'evidence obtained under different conditions cannot be comprehended within a single picture, but must be regarded as *complementary* in the sense that only the totality of the phenomena exhausts the possible information about the objects' (cited in Kumar, 2009, p. 242).

The complementarity principle states that the separate descriptions of the quantum realm obtained from different measurement events, or measured vs. unmeasured systems, cannot be combined into a single comprehensive description of reality. Rather, it is only possible to give a sequence of complementary descriptions which correspond to different measurement situations, or to the measured vs. the unmeasured system. Honner (1987, p. 59) refers to the type of complementarity that exists between the descriptions of a system corresponding to different measurement situations as 'weak' complementarity. For example, if a photon passes through a sequence of n polarizing discs then, to completely describe the photon's polarization with respect to each of the discs, it is necessary to give n distinct statements, all of which are complementary (rather than contradictory) to each other. Honner (1987, p. 59) contends, however, that the complementarity that exists between the descriptions of a measured vs. unmeasured system (e.g. the wave and particle manifestations of an electron corresponding, respectively, to the unmeasured and measured states of the electron), which he refers to as 'strong' complementarity, is more closely aligned with Bohr's original conception of complementarity. Accordingly, the analogue of strong complementarity in the study of psychological and educational predicates will be discussed in this section.

Wittgenstein (2009) demonstrated that there is a radical asymmetry between first-person present tense use and third-person present tense use of psychological concepts. First-person use and third-person use of mental predicates are asymmetrical with respect to their methods of verification since third-person use is based upon behavioural criteria, whereas first-person use is not. However, despite this asymmetry in their methods of verification, first-person and third-person use of mental concepts have, according to Wittgenstein, a univocity of meaning since they are linked to common behavioural criteria.

In Wittgenstein's view, asymmetry of use but univocity of meaning is a feature of all psychological predicates including intentional predicates such as thinking, learning, understanding and so on. For example, it is meaningful to speak of correct or incorrect in third-person use of the word 'ability', but it is meaningless to speak of correct or incorrect in first-person use of the word 'ability' (as there are no criteria to adjudicate on first-person use). Similarly third-person use of the word 'ability' is based on description, whereas first-person use is not, so that first and third-person uses of an intentional predicate are mutually exclusive. However, both first-person and third-person perspectives are necessary to give a full account of an intentional predicate. As Bohr noted, 'debates between behaviouristic and introspectivist positions in psychology can be resolved by recognising that both are necessary to complement each other for a full account of human experience' (Faye & Folse in Bohr, 1998, p. 19). First-person use of an intentional predicate precludes third-person use and the two uses are therefore not contradictory but, rather, complementary. Therefore, the asymmetry of first-person and third-person uses of intentional predicates, such as learning, is analogous to strong complementarity in quantum theory.

*The Analogue of Irreducible Uncertainty and Objective Probability*

Quantum theory cannot determine the exact behaviour of microentities but, rather, only permits probabilities of different possible outcomes to be calculated. Quantum uncertainty is irreducible in the sense that it cannot be reduced by acquiring further information about the system being considered, and the probabilities associated with the uncertainty are objective rather than subjective. The resort to probabilities is not associated with ignorance, and the irreducible uncertainty is simply a fact of the natural world. No theoretical approach has hitherto managed to circumvent the irreducible uncertainty in the quantum realm.

However, the situation in classical physics is very different from the quantum world. In classical Newtonian mechanics, it is only necessary to resort to probability when there is incomplete information regarding a particular system. Consider, for example, the situation that arises when an unbiased coin is tossed. If all of the parameters pertaining to the coin's motion were known, e.g. initial position, initial velocity, coefficient of restitution between the coin and the surface upon which it lands, were known, it would be possible to predict, with certainty, the outcome of the coin-tossing experiment (Strzalko, Grabski, Stefanski, Perlikowski, & Kapitaniak, 2008). In practice, however, at least some of these parameters will be unknown, and it is this 'classical ignorance' which leads to probabilities being invoked to describe the experimental outcomes. Probabilities of this type are subjective since the uncertainty with which they are associated would be reduced if further information were available. Indeed, with complete information regarding all of the parameters influencing the motion of the coin, the uncertainty would yield to certainty.

The Cartesian conception of the mind leads to the belief that, in the study of educational predicates such as thinking, the probabilities an individual associates with another person's thoughts are subjective, since the individual does not have direct access to the private mental states of the other person. Those aligned with the Cartesian view posit that there would be no uncertainty, and therefore, no need to resort to probabilities, if it were possible for the individual to have direct access to the mental states of the other person.

In Wittgenstein's rejection of Cartesianism, one's uncertainty in describing another person's mental states does not flow from ignorance of those mental states. According to Wittgenstein, when a person expresses a thought, for example, they are not giving voice to an inner state which the expression can be checked against for accuracy. Wittgenstein's private language argument rejects the existence of:

> ... a language in which a person could write down or give voice to his inner experiences—his feelings, moods, and so on ... The words of this language are to refer to what only the speaker can know—to his immediate private sensations. So another person cannot understand the language. (Wittgenstein, 2009, §243)

This suggests that the mental states of a person are not directly comparable with the person's subsequent actions and, therefore, that the uncertainty pertaining to the person's mental predicates cannot be reduced by inspecting their mental states.

Furthermore, if thoughts were self-contained, isolated brain processes that could be analysed using a brain imaging device, this would violate the characteristic first-person/third-person asymmetry which Wittgenstein (2009) identified as a feature of all mental predicates. First-person/third-person asymmetry refers to the fact that third-person ascriptions of psychological predicates are based upon the use of criteria, whereas first-person ascriptions are not. If the asymmetry is the defining property of the mental, then mental phenomena cannot be captured in brain processes:

> But the view that thoughts and feelings are brain-processes *abolishes* this logical difference. If this view were true, you and I would stand on the *same* level in regard to what I think and feel. In order to ascertain my thoughts and feelings you *and* I would equally have to rely on advanced technology and scientific theory. (Malcolm, 1986, p. 191)

Alas, physical entities such as brain processes are governed by first-person/third-person *symmetry* rather than asymmetry since both first-person and third-person ascriptions of physical predicates entail the invocation of criteria. 'After all, we say that Jones is six foot tall for the very same reason we say that we are' (Suter, 1989, p. 153). Entities characterized by first-person/third-person asymmetry cannot be construed as identical to entities characterized by first-person/third-person symmetry.

Therefore, the probabilities associated with mental predicates are objective, rather than subjective, since the uncertainty does not arise as a consequence of either human or instrumental limitations. Even if direct access to inner mental states were possible, it would reveal nothing and, consequently, the uncertainty associated with mental predicates is irreducible in the same way as the uncertainty in the quantum realm.

*The Analogue of Local Hidden Variables*

Einstein was an objective realist who believed strongly in a deterministic universe in which it is always possible to trace a clear path from local cause to effect. He refused to accept that quantum theory represents a complete fundamental theory of the natural world. A number of quantum theorists hold that Einstein insisted there must be 'elements of reality' which, if incorporated into quantum theory, would make it a more complete theory of physical reality. Einstein's 'elements of reality' are construed by physicists to refer to local hidden variables, i.e. Platonic 'look-up lists' which dictate the values of the dynamic attributes of a microentity in every possible measurement scenario. For example, according to Einstein, an unmeasured photon possesses a type of instruction list that identifies the photon's polarization along every possible angle before it is actually measured. However, Bell's theorem (Bell, 1964) proves conclusively that local hidden variables of this type do not exist.

Consider again an $n$-item mathematics test consisting of questions $Q_1$, $Q_2$, $Q_3$, ..., $Q_n$, where the response to each question is either correct or incorrect and suppose that an individual is about to answer a particular question $Q_r$ on the test. If the equivalent of Einstein's local hidden variables were to exist in the context of educational measurement, then the individual's ability with respect to $Q_r$ would be definite *in advance of* their answer to the question. In other words, the individual would have a hidden, internal 'look-up list' in their mind which would guide their response to $Q_r$. According to this view, whilst the assessor, due to their ignorance of these hidden variables, does not know how the individual will respond to $Q_r$ before it is actually answered, the individual's response could be predicted if this ignorance were eradicated. However, Wittgenstein's later philosophy suggests that such a view is implausible.

Wittgenstein counsels against looking for hidden causes of the behaviour associated with mental phenomena since he claims such a quest leads to conceptual confusion:

> Now we try to get hold of the mental process of understanding, which seems to be hidden behind those coarser, and therefore more readily visible, concomitant phenomena. But it doesn't work; or, more correctly, it does not get as far as a real attempt. For even supposing I had found something that happened in all those cases of understanding, why should that be the understanding? ... And if I say it is hidden—then how do I know what I have to look for? I am in a muddle. (Wittgenstein, 2009, §153)

In particular, he denies that the mental life of an individual is guided by latent, internal representations such as mental images. Wittgenstein concedes that mental images may be accompaniments of thinking, but he vehemently denies that such images actually *determine* how thoughts are expressed. If mental images were to determine the thinking of an individual, then Wittgenstein's paradox of interpretation (discussed in the section on rule following) would lead to the bizarre consequence that the individual in isolation might always be mistaken about their thoughts.

In Wittgenstein's (2009) view, a rule-follower is neither following a rule arbitrarily nor being guided by local hidden variables such as mental images. Rather, the rule-follower's guidance is non-local: their past training. The training is non-local since it is not stored inside the rule-follower as some form of mental object and hidden in the sense that the training itself (rather than its consequences) does not have any physical manifestation that is detectable by physically examining the rule-follower. Wittgenstein acknowledges that human beings have a repertoire of natural responses that can be moulded through training. However, he rejects the notion that training simply induces physical changes to neurological pathways in the brain that could be measured by an appropriate imaging device, since this would undermine the first-person/third-person asymmetry that is characteristic of psychological predicates (see above). Whilst changes to brain states obviously could be measured, the entity represented by the measurement would be governed by first-person/third-person symmetry and, therefore, it would be at variance with our common conception of psychological attributes. If one attempted to measure, for example, understanding using such advanced technology, the measurement would actually be of an entirely different predicate, understanding, say, that is incongruous with our everyday conception of understanding. Furthermore, as described in the section on rule following, Wittgenstein rejected the idea of a Platonic mechanism in an individual's mind that somehow gives access to all future applications of a rule.

Therefore, an individual who is just about to answer question $Q_r$ on the $n$-item mathematics test cannot be guided by some*thing* in mind; the individual does not have a hidden 'look-up list' that predetermines their answer to $Q_r$. Wittgenstein's philosophical discussions on the nature of meaning and understanding lead to the same conclusion for psychology and education as Bell's theorem led to for quantum theory: local hidden variables that guide behaviour are untenable.

The structural parallels that have been established between the study of educational/psychological predicates and quantum theory suggest that a quantum theoretical framework would provide a more secure philosophical basis for educational measurement than the Newtonianism that underpins contemporary measurement models. The essential features of this alternative measurement paradigm for educational predicates are summarized in the following section.

## Quantum Measurement Paradigm for Educational Predicates

Traditionally, educationalists have viewed measurement through a Newtonian lens, in the sense that measurement is construed as a process for checking up on an innate psychological attribute of a person: their ability. In the Newtonian tradition, ability is viewed as an intrinsic attribute of an individual which stands in a causal relation to their responses to the questions on a mathematics test, for example. The responses are judged to be 'correct' or 'incorrect' according to an independent standard that is external to the individual.

Consider again an $n$-item mathematics test consisting of questions $Q_1$, $Q_2$, $Q_3$, ..., $Q_n$, where the response to each question is either 'correct' or 'incorrect'. In the quantum theoretical framework for educational measurement, it is meaningless to speak of ability as an intrinsic property of an individual. Rather, it is only meaningful to refer to the individual's ability with respect to a given question at the instant when they actually respond to it. Therefore, an individual's responses to the $n$ questions will constitute $n$ discrete measurements of their mathematical ability with respect to each question.

Prior to measuring an individual's ability with respect to a given question, they are in a superposition of two states: their answer is both 'correct' *and* 'incorrect'. The superposition is ontological rather than epistemological. It is not that one does not know which state the individual is in, but they really *are* in both states simultaneously. When a measurement is made, the superposition collapses to yield one actual measurement result: the answer is either 'correct' *or* 'incorrect', and the uncertainty pertaining to which outcome will be actualized in the measurement process is irreducible. During the measurement, the individual and the measuring device, i.e. the practice assessed by the question, form a unified and non-separable system that actually influences the measured value of the ability.

If an individual answers all $n$ items on the hypothetical mathematics test, their ability will be definite on $n$ distinct occasions (when they are answering each of the $n$ items) and indeterminate between consecutive items (when they are not responding to a specific item). According to Bohr's principle of complementarity, it is necessary to give $n$ distinct descriptions (one corresponding to the individual's ability with respect to each test item) to completely capture the individual's mathematical ability. It is impossible to combine the $n$ statements since they are all necessary to give a complete description of the individual's mathematical ability. A consequence of this re-construal of educational measurement is that total test scores are meaningless since the rationale for summing item scores on a test is that each item is measuring the same construct, e.g. 'mathematical ability'. The scores cannot be combined in the quantum measurement paradigm because no single ability exists.

## Conclusion: Implications for Validity and the Future of Educational Measurement

Educationalists consider validity to be a critical issue in assuring the accuracy of the instruments which they use to measure ability levels. For example, in 1989, the British Psychological Society's Steering Committee on Test Standards defined validity as 'the extent to which a test measures what it claims to be measuring, the extent to which it is possible to make appropriate inferences from the test score' (cited in Coaley, 2009, pp. 129–130).

Educationalists contend that a test is valid if variations in the ability measured by the test are causally related to variations in the measurements derived from the test. The central tenet of validity in the context of educational measurement is the facility to abstract a measurement of ability away from the measuring instrument. The concept of validity evidently presupposes that an individual possesses an intrinsic ability level which is independent of the instrument used to measure it.

The quantum measurement paradigm presented in this article stresses that an individual's ability is actually a joint property of the individual and a particular test item. It is simply meaningless to divorce the ability from the measuring instrument. The author thus contends that the concept of validity as it is traditionally conceived in educational measurement is a misnomer.

The erosion of the notion of validity in educational measurement has grave implications for the legitimacy of the high-stakes assessments that currently dominate the educational landscape. Assessment results are, for example, used to award qualifications that determine future educational or vocational pathways of students. The results obtained by students in assessments are also used to gauge individual teacher quality, to hold schools to account for the standards achieved by their students, and to compare international education systems. Whilst it is acknowledged that transition to a quantum theoretical framework would not lead to the demise of educational assessment, the author believes that the focus on high-stakes assessments should be reduced. Ideally such assessments should be reformed to become as 'low-stakes' as possible through, for example, placing greater emphasis on qualitatively describing what students can do in particular contexts, rather than on attempting to quantify their educational achievements.

High-stakes assessments may, however, be justifiable in some contexts, despite the fact they do not yield valid measures of ability. There may still be strong links between a measurement produced by a test and a future expected outcome, which are useful for practical inductive reasoning, such as for making employment decisions, even if the test does not provide an accurate, ongoing, present-tense descriptor for the entity it purports to measure. It is the predictive strength of test scores that should determine if high-stakes assessments are justifiable in particular contexts. The ultimate consequence of the measurement model described in this article is to undermine some of the pro high-stakes assessment rhetoric that afflicts education, such as when authorities claim with an unjustifiably high degree of confidence what assessment data do or do not show, or they make epistemic claims about ability levels on the basis of test scores.

**Disclosure statement**

No potential conflict of interest was reported by the author.

**References**

Bell, J. S. (1964). On the Einstein Podolsky Rosen paradox. *Physics, 1,* 195–200.
Bohr, N. (1934/1987). *The philosophical writings of Niels Bohr volume 1: Atomic theory and the description of nature.* Woodridge, CT: Ox Bow Press.

Bohr, N. (1958/1987). *The philosophical writings of Niels Bohr volume 2: Essays 1933–1957 on atomic physics and human knowledge.* Woodridge, CT: Ox Bow Press.
Bohr, N. (1998). *The philosophical writings of Niels Bohr volume 4: Causality and complementarity* (Supplementary papers edited by J. Faye & H. J. Folse). Woodridge, CT: Ox Bow Press.
Boring, E. G. (1929). *A history of experimental psychology.* New York, NY: Century.
Bruner, J. (1996). *The culture of education.* Cambridge, MA: Harvard University Press.
Bruner, J. S. (1990). *Acts of meaning.* Cambridge, MA: Harvard University Press.
Coaley, K. (2009). *An introduction to psychological assessment and psychometrics.* London: Sage.
Gieser, S. (2005). *The innermost kernel.* Berlin: Springer-Verlag.
Gigerenzer, G. (1987). Probabilistic thinking and the fight against subjectivity. In L. Krüger, G. Gigerenzer, & M. S. Morgan (Eds.), *The probabilistic revolution – Volume 2: Ideas in the sciences* (pp. 11–33). Cambridge: The Massachusetts Institute of Technology Press.
Honner, J. (1987). *The description of nature: Niels Bohr and the philosophy of quantum physics.* Oxford: Oxford University Press.
Kripke, S. A. (1982). *Wittgenstein on rules and private language.* Oxford: Blackwell.
Kumar, M. (2009). *Quantum: Einstein, Bohr and the great debate about the nature of reality.* London: Icon Books.
Lagemann, E. C. (2000). *An elusive science: The troubling history of education research.* Chicago, IL: University of Chicago Press.
Malcolm, N. (1986). *Wittgenstein: Nothing is hidden.* Oxford: Blackwell.
Michell, J. (1990). *An introduction to the logic of psychological measurement.* Mahwah, NJ: Lawrence Erlbaum.
Michell, J. (1997). Quantitative science and the definition of measurement in psychology. *British Journal of Psychology, 88,* 355–383.
Michell, J. (1999). *Measurement in psychology: A critical history of a methodological concept.* Cambridge: Cambridge University Press.
Stapp, H. P. (1972). The copenhagen interpretation. *American Journal of Physics, 40,* 1098–1116.
Stevens, S. S. (1946). On the theory of scales of measurement. *Science, 103,* 677–680.
Strzalko, J., Grabski, J., Stefanski, A., Perlikowski, P., & Kapitaniak, T. (2008). Dynamics of coin tossing is predictable. *Physics Reports, 469,* 59–92.
Suter, R. (1989). *Interpreting Wittgenstein: A cloud of philosophy, a drop of grammar.* Philadelphia, PA: Temple University Press.
Wittgenstein, L. (1978). *Remarks on the foundations of mathematics* (G. H. von Wright, R. Rhees, & G. E. M. Anscombe, (Eds.), G. E. M. Anscombe, Trans., 3rd ed.). Oxford: Blackwell.
Wittgenstein, L. (1982). *Wittgenstein's lectures, Cambridge, 1930–1932: From the notes of John King and Desmond Lee* (D. Lee, Ed.). Oxford: Blackwell.
Wittgenstein, L. (2009). *Philosophical investigations: The German text with an English translation* (P. M. S. Hacker & J. Schulte, Eds., G. E. M. Anscombe, P. M. S. Hacker, & J. Schulte, Trans., 4th ed.). Chichester: Wiley-Blackwell.
Wright, C. (2001). *Rails to infinity.* Cambridge, MA: Harvard University Press.

# On the Un-becoming of Measurement in Education

NURAAN DAVIDS

## Abstract

*Education in democratic South Africa has been saddled with the extraordinary task of sanitising a once dehumanising and splintered education system into a singular narrative of social justice and creative, problem-solving individuals. This extraordinary effort has witnessed a pendulum swing from the openness of outcomes-based education, to a less flexible National Curriculum Statement, and recently, to what has been criticised as a too restrictive Curriculum Assessment Policy Statement (CAPS). In its narrow focus on 'assessment for learning', CAPS appears to be trapped in a particular understanding of teaching and learning that can be understood only in terms of measurement, thereby discounting education as happening outside that which can be measured. In this article, I contend, firstly, that while education is not averse to measurement, it cannot be allowed to dominate the educative process. Instead, it is possible to reconcile measurement, as expressed through a 'language of needs' with a language of 'coming into presence', which recognises that learners enter the education arena with their own ideas of what is known and yet to be known. Secondly, I argue, that if a post-apartheid education system hopes to re-humanise its citizens and society, then this will only be possible through cultivating a curriculum, which is understood as a process of socially just encounters—one which is always in becoming, and therefore not necessarily measurable.*

## Introduction

This article has two intertwining elements. One offers a glimpse into the still-unfolding story of curriculum reform and development since the emergence of a post-apartheid democratic South Africa. Here, I draw particular attention to the emphasis which is placed on practices of assessment, which I couch in terms of a language of measurement. The second theoretical element draws on Biesta's (2005) concepts of a language of needs and 'coming into presence'. While I draw a commonality between a language of measurement—as is propagated through the most recent South African curriculum policy—I extend the language of 'coming into presence' into a language of education that is always in becoming so that learners might learn, even when learning is not prescribed or held in check, through a prescribed set of assessment practices.

## Redressing a Post-apartheid Education System through Measuring the Needs of Learners

One of the main problems with the new language of learning, contends Biesta (2005, p. 55), is that it re-describes the process of education in terms of an economic transaction. As such, learners are viewed as consumers, whose particular needs are to be met by the teacher or educational institution. To reason that learners come to education with a clear understanding of their needs, says Biesta (2005, p. 59), is to both misconstrue the role of the teacher and the learner. To Biesta, such an understanding of education, described by him as a 'language of needs', not only defines education as a commodity, but seemingly fails to take into account who the learners are or what they bring. In its focus on education as a transactional engagement with learners, a language of needs forgets that one of the reasons for engaging in education is precisely to ascertain what the needs of learners might be. In other words, one of the goals of education is to encounter that which is yet to be encountered and known. If learners already know what they will encounter, the desire to pursue an education might be dramatically stifled. The parallel between a 'language of needs' and a language of measurement is that both are concerned with measuring only that which has been taught. Equally problematic about a language of needs, states Biesta (2005, pp. 59–60)—as it is about a language of measurement—is that it suggests a framework in which the only questions that can meaningfully be asked about education are those concerning the efficiency and effectiveness of the educational process and not about the content and purpose of education and its role in society.

Educational reform in post-apartheid South Africa has had to contend with similar concerns regarding its effectiveness, content and purpose, while simultaneously having to ensure that whatever changes are being implemented also address the inequalities of a historically racially biased education system. Redressing the education system in post-apartheid South Africa has been viewed as one of the major catalysts in restoring the values necessary for a socially just and democratic society. On the one hand, the newly elected democratic government was faced with the mammoth task of establishing a single national department of education out of 19 racially and ethnically divided departments of education. On the other hand, in recognising the key role of education in forging a fresh democratic identity and citizenship, the government was compelled to reform a deeply divisive and authoritarian national curriculum. Chisholm (2005, pp. 80–81) describes the politics that surrounded the curriculum revision—from 1994 to 2002—as being undertaken in three main stages or waves. The first involved the 'cleansing' of the curriculum of its racist and sexist elements in the immediate aftermath of the election—opening the door for outcomes-based education (OBE). With its non-prescriptiveness and reliance on teachers to create their own learning programmes, Chisholm (2005, p. 81) explains that the introduction of OBE was viewed as a pedagogical route out of apartheid education.

The objective with the implementation of OBE was to shift away from the apartheid education system (implemented in 1948), which was based on a particular Afrikaner form of Calvinistic principles, known as Christian National Education. While the warped basis of Christian National Education propagated that an individual's potential and opportunities were defined by race and ethnicity, it also placed the teacher at the centre of learning. This meant that while the teacher was considered as the sole authority of knowledge, learners were expected to listen, receive and memorise knowledge, without talking back. By contrast, OBE not only encouraged the learner to participate in her own learning, to think critically and to talk back, but positioned the teacher as the facilitator, rather than the authority of knowledge. In much the same way, then, that Christian National Education was used to distort identities and establish inequality, it was hoped that OBE would assist in establishing a new identity of parity. To this end, the openness and non-specificity in terms of teaching and learning of OBE was largely seen as the most appropriate vehicle through which to promote the ideals of a new democratic society.

However, three of the most significant criticisms, as voiced by Jansen (1998), questioned the political, epistemological and philosophical basis and desirability of OBE. Firstly, in raising political and epistemological objections to OBE, Jansen questioned how there could be such a strong focus on ends as final 'outcomes' when much of the educational and political struggle of the 1980s valued the processes of learning and teaching as ends in themselves (1998, p. 6). This criticism was exacerbated by the reality that the majority of teachers neither had access to information and resources nor understood OBE. Secondly, in questioning the philosophical justification of OBE in a democratic schooling system, Jansen pointed out that there was a fundamental contradiction in insisting that students use knowledge creatively only to inform them that the desired learning outcomes are already specified (1998, pp. 6–7). Thirdly, he contended that OBE's focus on instrumentalism—what a student can demonstrate given a particular set of outcomes—eluded not only the important issue of values in the curriculum, but eludes (still today), what education is for (1998, pp. 6–7). At the heart of Jansen's criticism is an echoing of Biesta's (2005) concern about what it actually is that schools are doing when their only concern is meeting the perceived needs of learners.

After 12 years of relentless criticism, frustration and disillusionment from teachers—supported by a dramatic decline in the average national pass rate of grade 12s from 60 to 40% over a ten-year period; concern about the exceptionally poor literacy and numeracy levels of primary school learners; and the dismal quality of passes in Mathematics and Science—OBE was finally re-considered in favour of a revised National Curriculum Statement (NCS) in 2002. In its proposal for the development of the NCS, the Report called for the promotion of social justice and equity through the development of creative, critical and problem-solving individuals (Chisholm, 2003). This was followed by the introduction of the Curriculum Assessment Policy Statement (CAPS), which according to the Department of Basic Education (DoBE, 2013), forms part of the NCS and aims to improve the quality of teaching and learning. In its focus on 'back to basics', CAPS offers a concise breakdown of what teachers need to teach and assess on a grade-by-grade and subject-by-subject basis—thus, in the opinion of the DoBE, ensuring that there is clear guidance and consistency for teachers when teaching. Problematically evident, however, in CAPS is disingenuous understanding of education as being entirely shaped by what it is that learners need to know.

**Assessment for Learning**

The most dramatic change brought about by CAPS has been its emphatic shift in focus from assessment *of* learning to assessment *for* learning. Evident in this shift is Biesta's (2005, p. 55) concern about the re-description of education as learning, as if learners need to only learn that which is to be assessed. While assessment of learning provides evidence of achievement for reporting purposes, assessment for learning provides information for the learner to facilitate future learning (Stiggins, 2002, p. 761). But, while the objective of assessment for learning might be to encourage learners to take responsibility for and reflect on their own learning, the levels of specificity in terms of content, as well as assessment practices of CAPS, have led to the curriculum being labelled as too prescriptive and restrictive (Ramatlapana & Makonye, 2012, p. 8).

Consider the following example of the teaching of languages in the Intermediate phase (grades 4–6). The learner is expected to acquire four skills, each of which has its own weighting: listening and speaking; reading and viewing; writing and presenting; and language structures and conventions. While 75% of learners' annual assessments are classroom based, 25% is based on a final-year exam. The classroom-based assessments are based on prescribed tasks, and each task is comprised of activities, which have to eventually constitute 75% of the learner's final result. There are two concerns about this type of approach. First is its lack of attention to the educative process, and, at times, the indeterminacy thereof. Secondly, education cannot only be understood as existing within that which is already known. Indeed, it is for this reason that after a class has been taught, and learners are asked to reflect on what they have learnt, some will respond with exactly what they have heard the teacher say, others will say they have learnt nothing and a few will say that they have learnt something which has in fact not been taught.

It is as important to understand why learners are measured, as it is to understand what it is that is being measured. Enter describes the measurement of learners as 'an investigation into the very ability of doing' (2007, p. 171). This description raises two points worth considering. On the one hand, one would need to understand what is meant by 'doing' inasmuch as one would need to wonder about that which is not being investigated. And on the other hand, if something is not being investigated, is the 'doing' still happening? If learners are being measured so that teachers might have a better sense of the ability of their learners, then, again, one needs to ask, whether what is being measured relates to what the learner has learnt or what the teacher has taught. Commonly, teachers measure only that which they have taught in the (often mistaken) belief that whatever they have taught must have been learnt by the learners. There are two assumptions here. Firstly, that the learner might not have learnt anything other than what has been taught, which explains why the teacher cannot measure what she has not taught. Secondly, that, learners do not learn by themselves —that is, in the absence of teaching or outside of the classroom. That learners might have learnt something other than what they were taught is seemingly not taken into account because the teacher has no real way of knowing what learners might have learnt other than what she has taught, unless she takes the time to gauge this from each of her learners. This in itself would require her to engage with her learners outside of that what she has taught.

On the one hand, the restrictive nature of OBE raised doubts about whether it could indeed achieve its intended objective of establishing a new identity of parity needed for the cultivation of a democratic and socially just society. On the other hand, the prescriptive nature of CAPS has brought into contention the initial democratic aims of OBE, which allowed the teacher the space to decide on her own content, sequencing the design of her own learning programmes, as well as assessment practices. So, from this perspective, the professional autonomy and creativity of teachers has been undermined (Reeves & McAuliffe, 2012, p. 10). Indeed, the uniform prescriptiveness of the CAPS curriculum has embargoed not only the space for any teacher's creativity, but has been boldly emphatic about what learners ought to learn, when they ought to learn it and how teachers are to measure whether this learning has taken place. In terms of the CAPS curriculum, assessment is understood as a process of collecting, analysing and interpreting information to assist teachers, parents and other stakeholders in making decisions about the progress of learners. As such, it serves to inform instruction; evaluate the effectiveness of teaching for all learners; assess learning; identify learner needs and strengths; and evaluate learner achievement against predetermined criteria for the purposes of grading and reporting (DoBE, 2013, p. 12). Moreover, while classroom assessment should be both informal and formal, learners should know what knowledge and skills are being assessed and feedback should be provided to learners after assessment to enhance the learning experience.

In returning to Biesta's (2005, p. 55) criticism of the rise of the concept of 'learning' at the expense of the concept of 'education', one has to question whether teaching and learning, which is predetermined by a language of measurement, can be considered as 'education'. To Peters (1966, p. 167), education is an initiation into activities which are worthwhile in themselves and which have certain cognitive features. Of course, education also involves measurement, such as educating someone in the Physical Sciences about exactitude and precision, and, of course, answers to a Mathematics or History test are either right or wrong—which means that measurement cannot simply be discounted. Education, however, cannot be constructed and contained in that which is measurable only because it discounts what happens outside of that which is being measured.

When the post-apartheid Department of Education called for the development of a Revised National Curriculum, it was done on the premise that education ought to encompass more than policy overload and limited transfer of learning into classrooms. Education, it was argued, should promote 'the values of a society striving towards social justice, equity and development through the development of creative, critical and problem-solving individuals' (Chisholm, 2005, pp. 82–83). This argument recognises that education needs to do something more than the transfer of knowledge. The

CAPS curriculum, however, with its predetermined emphasis on only that which can be measured, limits the educational process to a prescribed set of skills, which are held in check by a prescribed set of assessment practices. The educational process is limited because the presumption of CAPS is that if a learner efficiently and effectively answers some of the questions set in a particular test, then that learner has learnt successfully and the teacher has taught successfully. Whether the learner has been initiated into something, or desires to know something more or whether she has been provoked into questioning what is already known are discounted from the process.

In recognising that education is not averse to assessment, the next section argues for a correlative understanding between a language of measurement and Biesta's (2005) language of needs.

**A Language of 'Coming into Presence'**

What, then, would be an alternative to a language of measurement, so that a space is offered for that which is not predetermined? Stated differently, what does the CAPS curriculum need so that it addresses the needs of learners, while also addressing the content and purpose of education, as well as its role in society? The urgency of these questions has to be understood in relation to two critical discursive components of education in post-apartheid schools. One is the seemingly downward spiral in social values at South African schools. And the other is the confrontation of a majority school-leaving youth, who are neither skilled nor equipped to enter tertiary institutions or enter the workplace.

As an alternative to a language of needs, Biesta (2005, p. 62) suggests finding a language which allows the learner to show who she is and where she stands in relation to a social and intersubjective world—a language of 'coming into presence'. To 'come into presence', he explains, is to think of education as a process through which learners can come into a world where they encounter others, who are unlike them—so that they might find ways to respond to those who are different and so that they might see themselves in relation to others. This means that the learner would be encountering difference in the form of engaging with others, and by so doing, will encounter something yet to be known about herself, as well as others. In recognising the difference of others and the difference of the self in relation to others, the learner learns about her own autonomy and subjectivity, which therefore defines her singularity (Biesta, 2005, p. 62). She recognises that she cannot know about that which she has yet to encounter. In creating a situation where education is about the provision of opportunities for learners to encounter that which is unknown, the teacher cannot know what all the needs of her learners are and she cannot know everything that she has yet to teach. In this sense, education cannot only be linked to a predetermined curriculum, as CAPS sets out to do; education has to be taught and learnt in relation to that which is unexpectedly encountered in others and in oneself.

What sets a language of 'coming into presence' apart from a language of needs and measurement is, firstly, its acknowledgement that neither teachers nor learners can know what the education process holds. Secondly, being open to encountering difference and the unknown will necessarily mean being responsive to the unfamiliar. It is, of course, not possible to measure what learners are yet to encounter and how they will respond to this encounter. And, it is not possible for teachers to always know what the education process will hold since each learner brings her own subjectivity and presence to the classroom, inasmuch as teachers will respond differently to different encounters in the classroom. What a language of 'coming into presence', therefore, has on offer is an education which is non-measurable.

A language of needs as implicit in a language of measurement does not offer any unfilled spaces for the engagement of that which cannot be tested; it offers no gaps for that which might be desirable. Every space is already filled by what should be taught and what should be learnt, as if teaching and learning only happen in what is actually being taught and learnt. In focusing only on that which can be measured, a language of needs shuts itself off from the 'who' is being tested. Its only concern is the 'what'—since unlike the 'who', the 'what' is measurable. A language of needs and of measurement discounts that education does not happen only through that which is taught and learnt and it overlooks the space that is produced within and through the educational discourse. In acknowledging the 'who' of learners, Masschelein and Simons (2013, pp. 31–32) explain that the school, as an educational space (temporarily), creates the space and chance for learners to (temporarily) detach themselves from their circumstances (backgrounds, intelligence and struggles) and allows them to reflect upon themselves between where they are now and where they can be in the future. This is an especially valuable space for South African learners, who not only come from immensely varied social and economic backgrounds, but also learn in profoundly disparate schooling environments. To this end, while curriculum reforms speak to equality and representivity of all learners, the resources and opportunities available at post-apartheid South Africa have continued to be defined by a historical legacy of inequity. In countering these perceived limitations, Masschelein and Simons understand the school as, 'a means without an end, a vehicle without a determined destination' (2013, p. 36). Such an understanding not only offers hope, but as a vehicle without a determined destination, the school offers an open space for learners to 'come into presence'. The idea of a school without an end not only implies the idea of schooling being endless, and unconstrained by the physicality of a school, but also gives credence to a particular understanding of education—one which recognises education as an endeavour that requires continuous contestation and deliberation.

As Masschelein and Simons (2013, p. 60) observe, schools have, and continue to be accused of perpetuating social inequalities—and this would be true when encountered through a language of needs and measurement, as currently encapsulated in CAPS. However, in its space as 'a means without an end and a vehicle without a determined destination', education 'is the opening up of a world outside ourselves and the involving of the child or young person in that shared world' (ibid., 2013, p. 84). In order for learners to participate in, and engage with this shared world, they have to have a sense of who they are, so that they can come into presence and respond to others. If the process of education is understood as the pursuit of that which is yet to be commenced and encountered, then education is always beyond the now and what is already known—thereby contradicting a language of needs. This means that schools as spaces of pursuit have to equip learners how to be and how to be present in what Masschelein and Simons (2013, p. 84) describe as a shared world. If one considers that schools in South Africa have only been desegregated since 1992, and that the majority of schools have continued to retain their historical racial composition of learners—meaning that Black schools continue to serve only Black learners, and White schools White learners—then one begins to understand the urgent need for learners to be equipped how to be in a shared world. To be and to engage with others in a shared world means that learners will never be able to know all that there is to know of how to be with others and with difference. This is because the shared world, like the pursuit of education, exists along a continuum of encounters that cannot be known until it is encountered.

## A Language of Education in Becoming

In not offering a deliberative space for engagement or disruption, a language of needs belies the initiatory wonder of educational discourse and education. In contrast, a language of 'coming into presence' acknowledges the existence of difference and the yet to be known, and hence the wonderment of education. And yet the two languages of 'need' and 'coming into presence' might not necessarily be incommensurable. In other words, one does not have to dismiss one language over the other. Biesta's (2005) language of needs, while commensurable with measurement, is important as part of a social justice education. All learners need to have access to a particular type of teaching that will ensure a particular type of learning, so that all learners have access to the same set of opportunities. But, a language of needs cannot be allowed to dominate the educational discourse at the expense of offering learners the opportunity and space of 'coming into presence', so that they might enact their humanity towards themselves by recognising difference in others. The current situation in South African schools continues to be varied levels of access to opportunities, which continues to be defined along historically racial lines. Three cycles of curriculum reform have not been able to remedy this, which means that curriculum reform has to be approached via another avenue.

One of these avenues, and one of the ways for learners to be exposed to Biesta's (2005) language of 'coming into presence', is for teachers themselves to come into presence—not only through their teaching because learning is not necessarily dependent on teaching—but through their engagement with learners. When teachers come into the presence of learners, they present themselves as part of the educational discourse, rather than standing outside of it. They therefore insert themselves into the uncertainty and openness of what it means to educate and to be educated. They present themselves in duality—as those who have come to teach and learn, and they acknowledge that they neither know all there is to know about their subject nor what the needs of their learners are. This means that teaching is not only about the 'what', as CAPS deems education to be. Education is about the 'who' and the 'how'—meaning who the teachers and learners are, and 'how' teachers engage with learners and how learners engage with others. To this end, education is always determined by who the learners and teachers are and by how the education is allowed to unfold. It is for this reason that two teachers can teach the same lesson, but their learners will have two different sets of experiences

—based on the extent to which the teacher has either held onto the 'what' or the extent to which she has allowed the 'who' and the 'how' to emerge, develop and reveal the educative process. As such, I wish to argue that education is indeed not only about 'coming into presence'—that education is more than a process of encounters. It is also about that which is yet to happen, yet to be known and seen.

In drawing on the thoughts of Masschelein and Simons (2013, p. 36), education has no end. As such, education is always in becoming because teachers and learners have no real way of knowing how the educative process will unfold and what will be revealed. What an education in becoming does for teaching and learning is that, on the one hand, it acknowledges the space necessary for encounters with the unknown —in terms of subject content and in terms of encountering the other. And, on the other hand, it recognises that part of the educative process has to be left to the unplanned, the unmeasured and be left to that which hankers beyond which is yet to be known. In attempting to know (and measure) everything, the educative process is no longer in becoming. Education has to be understood as happening everywhere, all the time. What remains for the teacher is to listen to the desires of her learners, so that they are led to understand that education is unconfined by the walls of a classroom. Education, therefore, is always in becoming; it is not fixed in time or space or limited to one particular understanding. It straddles simultaneous initiatory processes: one which ensures that learners are equipped with the necessary skills and training so that they are initiated into becoming active, participatory, critical-thinking and contributing beings; and the other which recognises that education is not limited to the now and the known.

Education in becoming, like an education of coming into presence, recognises that learners, as human beings, are firstly, constituted by the 'who', which means that their humanity, their curiosities and their desires cannot be discounted from the educative process. To this end, an education in becoming needs to be facilitated through a particular understanding of democracy—one that focuses on being open to the views of others, such as the teacher being open to the desires of the learner. Instead, then, of a democracy that is only understood in terms of rights, what I am arguing for is a democracy that is receptive to being talked back to—in other words, being open to the words of others and the otherness of others.

To be receptive and responsive to others in a shared world means more than just engaging with difference; it also means to be willing to listen, to be swayed by the opinions of others, and at times, to concede to the arguments of others. It also means listening to views, which might not be considered as desirable or downright offensive. Like elsewhere in the world, where oppression has dehumanised and demoralised certain groups of people, based on race, ethnicity or religion, South African society has struggled in connecting with the other, largely due to the fracturing effects of apartheid. Consequently, it is not uncommon for both learners and teachers to refer to other learners using derogatory terms or language. Unless a post-apartheid curriculum and schools offer the spaces where these forms of undesirable speech can be discussed and debated, they will continue. In this instance, I am in agreement with the view expressed by Butler (1997, pp. 129–133), who argues that attempts to censor particular forms of undesirable speech, such as hate speech, propagates the very speech it intends to repress. She contends that by listening to undesirable speech, it is possible for the speech to become disjoined from their power to hurt and 're-signified' into a more affirmative mode. This type of engagement, which is based on listening without prejudice, offers a particular enactment of democracy. It understands being open to the otherness of others, not so much by the extent to which we are prepared to recognise difference, but by the extent to which we are prepared to see ourselves as different to others, rather than others being different to ourselves. In recognising our own difference and our own otherness, we become open to the possibility that somebody else might have something worthwhile to say, and that co-existence in a shared world has less to do with one's own rights than it has in affording others the right to speak to us and to shift us in our thinking. Teachers, in this instance, instead of teaching only in terms of a language of needs and measurement ought to also teach in terms of a language which facilitates listening to the views of others. This includes teachers listening to what their learners have to say, understanding what they might find desirable, as well as creating a classroom environment where learners listen to and learn from their peers. In a shared world like this, learners bear testimony to a particular enactment of humane engagement and democracy, in the sense that each of us has the right to be heard and should therefore be listened to.

Of course, as stated previously, education straddles and connects multiple initiatory processes—and enacting our humanity in a shared world, albeit the most important, is just one part of it. In order to become active participants in a shared world requires more than just recognition of the self and of others. It is also about having the necessary skills and training to become productive and worthwhile members of society—as encompassed by a language of needs. South African society is aware of the reality that had the current national pass rate as 50%, instead of 40%, only 24% of grade 12s would have passed their exams. A 24% pass rate does not speak to a skilled or educated school-leaving population. Education means that learners ought to know certain facts, own certain skills and have an awareness of certain ideas. Similarly, they ought to be acquainted with the art of debate, and be capacitated to leave the shared world of schooling with a clear sense that their education has only just begun. What this means is that they have to be awakened to the world around them, so that they are equipped to navigate their own path and become. Education in becoming means that not only is the destination never reached, but that the destination itself cannot always be predetermined. To be open to the otherness of others, therefore, also means being open to oneself and one's path in a shared world.

In concluding, it is possible to reconcile a language of needs and of measurement, as is found in CAPS, with a language of 'coming into presence', which recognises that learners come into a shared world where they encounter the unknown. Education as a process cannot only be understood in terms of an end or in terms of that which can be measured. Education has to be understood in terms of a continuum—where learners are offered the spaces, where they might encounter the unknown, but are also allowed to move back on the continuum so that they might re-consider that which they have always held to be true, or right or wrong. So, on the one hand, while measurement might offer the motivation necessary to learn, measurement in itself is not educational. On the other hand, however, being open to others is certainly worth achieving—both in the means, and as an end, in terms of societal good and democracy. Education happens when learners are initiated into themselves, and they are prepared to present those selves to others and are prepared to have others presented to themselves, so that they might better engage in a shared, yet contested world. The greater the coming into presence, the greater the responsiveness to others, and therefore the greater the opportunity for educational encounters. If the objective of the post-apartheid education system was to 'cleanse' the curriculum of its dehumanising elements, then the only way to re-humanise it is through a cultivation of a curriculum and an educational process, which is humane and is based on the values of social justice.

This article has argued that the prescriptive focus on 'assessment for learning' has trapped the recently introduced CAPS curriculum in a particular understanding of teaching and learning that can be understood only in terms of assessment and measurement. This prescriptive focus has not only impeded teacher autonomy and creativity, but has stifled the spaces of potentiality which education ought to be offering to learners. While education is not averse to measurement, the latter cannot be allowed to dominate the educative process, as is currently being experienced by South African teachers, following the CAPS curriculum. Instead, this article has argued that it is possible for measurement, as expressed through a language of needs, to reconcile with a language of 'coming into presence'. This reconciliation is possible when education is understood as more than a process of encounters, but also as that which is yet to happen and yet to be known—hence, an education in becoming.

**Disclosure statement**

No potential conflict of interest was reported by the author.

**References**

Biesta, G. J. J. (2005). Against learning, reclaiming a language for education in an age of learning. *Nordisk Pedagogik, 25*, 54–66.

Butler, J. (1997). *Excitable speech: A politics of the performative.* New York, NY: Routledge.
Chisholm, L. (2003). *The politics of curriculum review and revision in South Africa.* Presented at the Oxford International Conference on Education and Development, 9–11 September 2003 at the session on Culture, Context and the Quality of Education, Oxford University, Oxford.
Chisholm, L. (2005). The politics of curriculum review and revision in South Africa in regional context. *Compare, 35,* 79–100.
Department of Basic Education. (2013). *Curriculum and assessment policy statement.* Pretoria: Government Printers.
Enter, S. (2007). *Spel.* Amsterdam: G. A. van Oorschot.
Jansen, J. D. (1998). Curriculum reform in South Africa: A critical analysis of outcomes-based education. Retrieved February 20, 2014, from http://hdl.handle.net/2263/132
Masschelein, J., & Simons, M. (2013). *In defence of the school: A public issue.* (J. McMartin, Trans.). Leuven: Education, Culture and Society Publishers.
Peters, R. S. (1966). *Ethics and education.* London: George Allen & Unwin Ltd.
Ramatlapana, K., & Makonye, J. P. (2012). From too much freedom to too much restriction: The case of teacher autonomy from National Curriculum Statement (NCS) to Curriculum and Assessment Statement (CAPS). *African Education Review, 9,* 7–25.
Reeves, C., & McAuliffe, S. (2012). Is curricular incoherence slowing down the pace of school mathematics in South Africa? A methodology for assessing coherence in the implemented curriculum and some implications for teacher education. *Journal of Education, 61,* 6–11.
Stiggins, R. (2002). Assessment crisis: The absence of assessment for learning. *Phi Delta Kappan, 83,* 758–765.

# Index

Note: Page numbers followed by "n" denote endnotes.

ACARA *see* Australian Curriculum, Assessment and Reporting Authority (ACARA)
'age of measurement' 4–7, 20
AITSL *see* Australian Institute for Teaching and School Leadership Limited (AITSL)
Anderson, E. 39, 48n2
Anheier, H. K. 65n15
apartheid education system 113; *see also* post-apartheid education system
Apple, M. W. 24
Aquinas T. 59–60
Arab Spring 52
Aristotle 12, 59, 75; *Nichomachean Ethics* 52; *Politics* 59, 65n10
artistic/aesthetic knowledge 75, 76
Ashton, D. 26
assessment 3, 68–70; classroom-based 114; educationally significant learning 73–6; formative 74; knowledge and education 70–3; for learning 114–16; summative 74
Augustine 87, 88
Augustinian pedagogy 86
Australian Curriculum, Assessment and Reporting Authority (ACARA) 25
Australian Institute for Teaching and School Leadership Limited (AITSL) 20

Barnett, R. 26, 27, 30, 31
Bauman, Z. 22
behaviourism, cognitivism and 97, 99
Beitz, C. 46–7
Belenky, M. F. 25, 26
Bell's theorem 106
Biesta, G. J. J. 2, 20–3, 29, 31, 32, 111, 112, 114–16, 118
Big Data 2, 81, 82
Blake, N. 23
Bohman, J. 47
Bohr, N. 3, 94–7, 99, 100, 104; principle of complementarity 103–4, 108

Boring, E. G. 96
British Psychological Society 108
Brown, P. 26
Bruner, J. S. 96
Butler, J. 119–20

Cantley, Ian 2
capability approach 40–2
CAPS *see* Curriculum Assessment Policy Statement (CAPS)
Carr, D. 71, 72, 75
charitable organizations 44
children's labor 37
Chisholm, L. 112
Christian National Education 113
civic associations 58, 59, 64n8
civil society 2, 53–9; associational life in 58; civics and 55, 59; conceptions of 54, 56–7; human identity 59–61; measurement and educational aims 61–3
classroom-based assessments 114
Clinchy, B. M. 25
closed-systems approach 25
Cohen, Julie 81
'coming into presence,' language of 116–18
complementarity principle 103–4
*Concept of Mind* (Ryle) 65n14
Confucian education 60
Confucianism 2, 63
Confucian philosophy 60
contemporary educational measurement models 94–5; educational predicates (*see* educational predicates); psychology's 'physics envy' 95–7
contemporary educational systems 53; measurement regime on 5; precursory survey of 1
Copenhagen interpretation of quantum theory 97
cosmopolitan democracy 47
culture of measurement 12–13

'currency of justice' 40
Curriculum Assessment Policy Statement (CAPS) 113–17, 120
'customers of education' 69

Davis, A. 69–70, 74
democracy 2, 16, 33, 56, 119–21; cosmopolitan 47
democratic professionalism 13–17
democratic schooling system, outcomes-based education in 113
democratisation of professions 7–8
Department of Basic Education (DoBE) 113
Department of Education 115
Descartes, R. 2, 85–7, 89, 90
*Development as Freedom* (Sen) 42
Dewey, J. 21–3, 26, 30, 32; ends-in-view 2, 27–9; intellectual factor 31; theory of valuation 29
Digital Taylorism 26
dissatisfaction, with life and cynicism 52
DoBE *see* Department of Basic Education (DoBE)
Donskis, L. 22
Dretske, F. 83

Early Childhood Development 24
economic development, policy and practice in 45
educational epistemology 72
educational institutions 52, 54
educational predicates 99–100; complementarity principle 103–4; Heisenberg's uncertainty principle 101; irreducible uncertainty and objective probability 104–6; local hidden variables 106–7; quantum measurement paradigm for 107–8; quantum theory 100–1; wave function collapse 101–3
educational reform, in post-apartheid South Africa 112
Education for All 37, 44; *Global Monitoring Reports* 43
education, liberal conceptions of 81
effective learning 27
Einstein 43, 106
'Embodied learning' (Stolz) 78n6
Enslin, P. 2
epistemology, educational 72
evidence-based practice, professional knowledge to 11–12
evidence constraint 71

fairness function 40
Feinberg, W. 9
'feminization of global poverty' 42
Feyerabend, P. 21

Floridi, Luciano 86
formative assessment 74
Fromm, Eric 22, 29

General Definition of Information 84–5
GFC *see* Global Financial Crisis (GFC)
Giddens, A. 22
Gingell, J. 69–70
Giroux, H. 22, 30
givenness 81, 85, 88, 89
global civil society 54
global educational opportunity: counted count 43–4; disaggregating global political structures 46–7; justice 38–43; measurement, use and misuse of 36–8; poor count 45–6; redistribution 44–5; structural change 45
Global Financial Crisis (GFC) 56
*Global Monitoring Reports* 43
global poverty 37, 45; feminization of 42
Goldberger, N. R. 25
Gramsci, Antonio 53, 55–8, 63, 64n7

Habermas, J. 56–7
Hardie, C. D. 62
HDI *see* Human Development Index (HDI)
Heideggerian phenomenology 88
Heisenberg's uncertainty principle 101
Heisenberg, Werner 97
Held, D. 47
Hirst, P. H. 71
Honner, J. 103
'human capital' 69
Human Development Index (HDI) 37, 42, 43
*Human Development Reports* 42, 43, 45, 46
human identity 59–61, 64n2

individual educators, role of 21–3
inequalities, in educational opportunities 38
informational-causal chain 87
information systems 83–5
information-theoretic conception 83–5
INGOs *see* International Non-government Organisations (INGOs)
insecurity 51, 52
instability 51
integrated global economy 46–7
intermediate phase 114
international non-government organisations (INGOs) 54, 64n3
international poverty line (IPL) 48n3
International System of Units (SI) 1
intrinsic givenness 88
irrevocable givenness 88
item response theory 95

Jansen, J. D. 113
Jarvis, P. 74

# INDEX

The Journal of Educational Psychology (Thorndike) 24
justice, global educational opportunity: morally plausible metrics 42–3; objectivity and metrics 41; preliminaries 38–9; resources/capabilities 39–41

Kelly, E. 41
Kennedy, Robert 61–2, 65n13
Kierkegaard, S. 23, 29, 30, 32
knowledge: artistic/aesthetic 75, 76; and education 70–3; mechanistic approach to 83; objective 72, 77; practical 74, 76, 78n8; professional 6, 11–12; propositional 74, 76; rich 74, 76; theoretical 76; tripartite structure of 86
Kongzi (Confucius) 65n11, 65n12
Kripke, S. A. 102

Lagemann, E. C. 95
language of education 118–21
large-scale public testing 70, 74, 75
Latour, B. 5
Lauder, H. 26
learning analytics 2, 80; design processes and theories of learning 81; ethical consideration of 82; information-theoretic conception 83–5; intentional subject, learner as 85–90
Lewis, D. 64n8
life expectancy 37
Light, M. 37
Lundie, D. 2
Lyotard, J.-F. 24

MacIntyre, A. 55, 72, 78n5
Mackay, Tony 20
Marion, Jean-Luc 2, 85–8
Masschelein, J. 117, 119
means–end dichotomy 24
measuring practices 3, 20–1; current culture of measurement 23–4; educating our desires 29–32; individual educators, role of 21–3
*Meditatio II* (Descartes) 85, 86
Meirieu, P. 15
Metre Convention 1
metric of justice 39–40, 43
Michell, J. 95–6
Millennium Development Goals 37, 44
'mineness' 89
Moore, A. 74
morally plausible metrics 42–3
Mouffe, Chantal 16
My School website 69, 70

National Assessment Programme—Literacy and Numeracy (NAPLAN) 25, 28, 69, 70, 74, 76
National Curriculum Statement (NCS) 113

natural-language-use test 84
Newtonian mechanics 104
Newtonian physics 95, 96
*Nichomachean Ethics* (Aristotle) 52
Noddings, N. 23
non-government organisations (NGOs) 45, 54, 58; *see also* international non-government organisations (INGOs)
normative validity 5, 10, 21, 29
Nussbaum, M. 2, 40, 43, 45, 47, 48n4

Oakeshott, M. 73
OBE *see* outcomes-based education (OBE)
objective knowledge 72, 77
Okin, S. M. 42, 45, 46
O-Neill, Onara 10–11
Open Method of Coordination 47
oppression 51, 119
Organisation for Economic Co-operation and Development 77n2
outcomes-based education (OBE) 112–13; in democratic schooling system 113; restrictive nature of 115

Parfit, D. 47n1
performativity 5
Perry, W. G. 26, 29; intellectual and ethical development 32
personal identity, development of 53
Peters, M. A. 20
Peters, R. S. 62, 71, 115
Philosophy of Education Society of Australasia (PESA) 2
'physics envy' 95–7
Plato 70–3
Platonic epistemology 74–5
Platonic mechanism 98
Pogge, T. 37–9, 41, 43–7, 48n2, 48n3
political association 58
*Politics* (Aristotle) 59, 65n10
positivist epistemology 83
post-apartheid education system 112–14
post-democratic distortions 8–12; from client/patient/student to customer 9–10; democratic to technical-managerial accountability 10–11; professional knowledge to evidence-based practice 11–12
poverty 37, 43–6, 48n3, 51–2; *see also* global poverty
practical knowledge 74, 76, 78n8
Pring, R. 24
private association 58
professionalism, traditional configuration of 7
professional knowledge 6, 11–12
propositional knowledge 74, 76
pseudo-security 6

# INDEX

psychological constraint 71
Putnam, H. 21

'quality teaching' 22
quantum measurement paradigm 109; for educational predicates 107–8
quantum theory 100–1, 104, 106

radical givenness 88
Rawlsian metric 40
Rawls, J. 39–41, 46, 47, 55
Rawls's theory 40
redistribution, global educational 44–5
resourcist approach 41
responsibility 89
Revised National Curriculum 115
rich knowledge 74, 76
Roberts, P. 20
Ryle, G. 65n14

'scientific task' 95
Scott, J. 37
Selwyn, N. 82
Sen, A. 2, 39, 40–2, 47, 48n2
Simons, M. 117, 119
Skinner, B. F. 73
Smeyers, P. 23
Smith, R. 23
social justice 2
social psychology, of measurement regime 6
Socrates 70–1
Standish, P. 23
Steering Committee on Test Standards 108
Stevens, S. S. 96
Stolz, S. A. 2, 78n6
structural change, global educational 45

structural reforms 45
summative assessment 74
symbol-grounding approach 84, 89

Tarule, J. M. 25
Taubman, P. M. 23–4
Taylor, C. 22
teacher assessment 68
'teaching-to-the-test' syndrome 69, 78n3
technical-managerial accountability, democratic to 10–11
technical validity, of measurements 5
*Theaetetus* (Plato) 70
theoretical knowledge 76
theories of justice 39
Thorndike, Edward 24
Tjiattas, M. 2
Tomazin, F. 78n4
townspeople 55
truth constraint 71

United Nations Development Program (UNDP) 42
utilitarianism 38, 40, 47n1

wave function collapse 101–3
Webster, R. S. 2
Wilde, Oscar 4
Winch, C. 69–70, 74, 75
Wischermann, J. 57
Wittgenstein, L. 3, 95, 97, 103–4, 106; Cartesianism, rejection of 105; psychological attribute 100; rule following analysis 97–9, 107; wave function collapse 102

Young, I. M. 44, 58, 64n9